Carnie

CARNIE

by Les Bodnar

ST. AUGUSTINE'S PRESS
South Bend, Indiana

Manufactured in the United States of America

1 2 3 4 5 6   15 14 13 12 11 10

Library of Congress Cataloging in Publication Data
Bodnar, Les.
    Carnie / by Les Bodnar.
        p. cm.
    Includes bibliographical references and index.
    ISBN 978-1-58731-101-7 (hardbound: alk. paper)
    1. Bodnar, Les. 2. Carnival owners – Middle West.
    3. Circus performers –Middle West. 4. Carnivals –
    Middle West. I. Title.
    GV1834.72.B64A3 2010
    791.10973 – dc22   2010027394

∞ *The paper used in this publication meets the minimum requirements of the American National Standard for Information Sciences - Permanence of Paper for Printed Materials, ANSI Z39.48-1984.*

ST. AUGUSTINE'S PRESS
www.staugustine.net

Contents

Acknowledgments

THE IMPETUS TO WRITE "CARNIE" BEGAN WITH THE DESIRE of my family to know more of my early life, especially that life with the carnival. Susan and Mary Pat pushed me; Julianne, Kathy, and Beth encouraged me; and the boys, Tom, Jim, Bill, and Michael, critically assessed the work. Even my wonderful wife, gone now for ten years after fifty-six good ones, had not heard all of this story. My youth was a revelation to all of them, just as it seems to be to everyone.

They all have difficulty believing that I, a serious orthopaedic surgeon in my busy real life, in which they had known me only as a distant dad, could have been the kid living in the carnival world, amidst all the trappings and traps, snares and seductions, glamour and gaffs, of the unreal life of the "carnie."

However, once I started to write, the thoughts and memories began to return. When they were incomplete or inadequate, a touch of fiction here and there filled the void, easily occasioned by the eighty-year interval between the events and the current times. As a result, times, persons, and places really became jumbled, but since only you and I are aware of that, I allowed the story to run on its own.

An example of that is the Klu Klux Klan episode which

really occurred in 1924, according to the findings of my research. I was only eight years old then, yet the memory of that burning of the crosses by hooded men is still vivid in my memory.

In researching certain facets of the story, hoping to verify the facts, I encountered many helpful people, eager to share in developing the project. Librarians, carnival workers, historians, clerks in city and county offices, and others, did their best to assist me.

One of the amusing situations was that which occurred when I was trying to verify the church for which we played when the "42 Gang" was paid off to protect us as we played that Italian Festival in Chicago. I contacted several churches in that area before I located a Catholic priest who seemed to recall that some church, which by now had been demolished, in that blighted area of Chicago, did have such a festival each year, but he was too young to recall much about it. However he did have an elderly parishioner, "Stella," who "might know," he said. I phoned Stella and was informed she was not at home and what did I want with her? It took some coaxing to gain the confidence of the speaker but ultimately she gave me the information I needed, further confiding that she was indeed Stella and I was not to tell anyone who gave me the information. I guess it's still best to keep your mouth shut in that neighborhood.

On my visits to various outfits and organizations in the last few years, I made some interesting friends and contacts who willingly and almost eagerly related their experiences and the conduct of today's carnivals. I am grateful to these many good people who brought me up to date on their world as it now exists.

"Butch" Butler, owner of Butler Amusements, was

my initial personal contact with the principals of today's carnivals, and whose graciousness encouraged me to write a final chapter on the carnival of today to complete my book, *"Carnie."*

Sonja Schetman, of the Stripes Unit of North American Midway Entertainments, is its competent woman manager, married, raising her family of two children while on the road. She was most cooperative in answering my querries on today's shows.

Danny Huston, CEO of North American Midways Entertainment, and his son, Blake, who operates the Stars Unit of the shows, are two Hoosiers whom I met while they were playing local fairs. Both are classy people, originating in central Indiana farm country.

Ward Hall, Chris Christ, and Pete Terhune, are the ultimate showmen, who were most hospitable to me when I visited them in "Gibtown."

Joe Skerbeck, owner and manager of one of the units of the Skerbeck Brothers shows, and his son, Jamie, and wife, Sonja, were most amiable and forward in detailing the activities of their outfits. They are members of a wide family involvement in the carnival world.

Patti McClain, of the North American Midway Entertainment Shows, was a most cooperative young woman doing her job as public relations officer with her outfit.

Charles Panacek Jr., the owner of the Belle City Amusements, a well-run family operation for well over fifty years, also gave me good information.

Kenneth Hayward is the owner of Wabash Valley Shows, one of the smaller outfits I visited. His is another outfit passing through several generations of one family.

"Corky" Daniel is the competent manager of one of the units of the Wade Shows, owned by Fred Zaitshik.

Bob Johnson is president and CEO of the Outdoor Amusement Business.

John Drummey, executive secretary, and Diana Burmeister, his assistant, are in the offices of the Showmen's League of America.

Steve Ianni is president of the International Independent Showmen's Association.

I would especially like to acknowledge the good advice of publisher Kathleen Hughes of Capital Books, who spoke to me early on of my attempt at writing a book, keeping my expectations in proper perspective, warning of the trials ahead, and Diane Altorfer who taught me tricks on my computer and dutifully proof-read the ensuing results.

And, of course, I am deeply indebted to Bruce Fingerhut, for his careful editing and sound advice on my manuscript and the publication of this book.

The song "Ramona" was written by L. Wolfe Gilbert, with music by Mabel Wayne in 1927.

There were others. I am grateful to all of them for their help in this effort which I hope will be entertaining and informative to all who are curious about this interesting way of life. And it was an interesting life. And I lived it: the life of a "Carnie."

Lexicon of Terms Used by "Carnies"

Bally: the presentation on the bally platform in front of a show.

Blow-off: the big special show, an extra attraction, for suckers.

Carnie: a carnival worker or a fan of the carnival world

Cookhouse: the food service area primarily for the carnival folks.

Flash: the bright and showy presentation of a unit or of game prizes.

Front-speaker or talker: the person conducting the bally.

Geek: the "wild man." impersonator.

Gimmick or gaff: the means of operator control of games of chance.

Grab Joint: a quick food concession, usually a stand-up food service.

Grifter: operator of a crooked game.

Grind: the steady spiel or talk by showman to attract interest in the show.

Hey Rube: the call when a fight may erupt with the "marks."

Inside speaker, talker, lecturer: he person conducting the show inside.

Joint:	a carnival concession.
Jump:	the move from one location to the next.
Lot:	the carnival grounds.
Mark:	town person, customer, or player at a game.
Midway:	the area along which the carnival's attractions are aligned.
Move:	the move of the entire carnival to its new location.
Nut:	operating expenses.
On the road:	traveling with the carnival.
Outfit:	refers to the entire carnival, sometimes to only a unit of same.
Play:	to operate the carnival at some location.
Ride:	Unit of carnival providing thrilling experience in motion.
Route:	the circuit of locations at which the carnival will operate.
Set-up:	to erect the components of the carnival.
Shill or stick:	a person with the carnival who appears to be a towns-person or "mark" luring others to play a game of chance.
Show:	usually refers to the entire carnival, but may be in reference to a unit of the carnival to be viewed for entertainment.
Slum:	cheap prizes.
Spot:	also the carnival grounds.
Tear-down:	to dismantle the carnival.
Throw a cop:	to conduct the game so the "mark" wins.
Tip:	the crowd gathering to hear the bally.
With it:	expression used to indicate that one is a carnie.

Foreword

"CARNIE" IS A MEMOIR, RELATED AS A STORY, MOSTLY TRUE, based on events in my life as a boy of almost twelve years of age, when the story begins in 1928, the son of the owner of a traveling carnival, playing the Chicago and Midwest areas. In this, I rely on my recollections of those events with a memory which, at my age of ninety-four years, is riddled with holes similar to that of Swiss cheese. Therefore, this is compensated for by considerable embellishment of the facts, and some events are the product of imagination based on a scarcity of facts as well as on hearsay and faulty memory surrounding certain episodes. Some of the story is pure fiction. However the events actually occurred. Sometimes time and place are repositioned to provide a moving vehicle for the story which is otherwise woven into an autobiographical rendition, a memoir, of the events and of the times.

So, I beg the reader to accept a certain degree of license to be inaccurate in some details, a matter which I feel to be my privilege when one considers the passage of the many years between the occurrences related and the time of relating these events. So said, I am hopeful that you will find this interesting and entertaining, as well as a well-disguised morality story. Now, that is stretching it a bit, isn't it? Carnivals and morality? An oxymoron? We'll see.

Carnies

My earliest recollection of the carnival was that of being put to sleep in the light box of the Merry Go-Round, on a blanket over a pile of excelsior for a bed. I was about five or six at the time, and it was past bedtime. It was spring and the night was chilly. It was probably our usual opening "spot" in Gary, Indiana. It's strange that I can remember that particular occasion, one of the earliest memories of my youth.

The light box, filled with excelsior, was probably about three by five feet and three feet deep. The excelsior, wood curlicue shavings, was the soft material before the days of styrofoam and bubblewrap used for storing the hundreds of light bulbs illuminating the inner and outer panels of the Merry-Go-Round. The box had been placed near the gasoline engine which powered the "ride," giving off heat, making it a cozy spot for me.

It was dizzying to look up and see the wooden horses and the lights whirling around above me while the organ rasped out its melody with an occasional wheeze when a valve failed, accompanied by the cymbals and drum at each end of the massive organ.

As I lay there in my light-box crib, about to go to sleep, I heard voices near me. Slim, who ran the Merry-Go-Round, was to keep an eye on me.

Slim, was a tall, lanky guy, who always wore a cowboy hat, high-heeled boots, and chewed on match sticks. He was rather typical of a good number of our carnival workers. They didn't expect much out of life, changed occupations quite often, were frequently on the move, made do with whatever the circumstances dictated, managed somehow under even difficult conditions, worked as hard and reliably as was required from time to time without overdoing it, and were of limited education, ambition, and means.

Slim had been standing next to my crib when he threw in the clutch to start the ride. He gradually increased its tempo to the usual and timely gallop until his horses were prancing along at a merry but safe pace. Swede, his helper, would collect tickets from the riders. It took only two men to operate the ride, and another one sold tickets. John De-Jung, who owned the ride, usually sold tickets except when his wife, Frieda, came out. She must have been selling that day because I could hear John talking. Slim had just told John of a problem. Slim spoke with a drawl.

"John, there's somep'n wrong with one of them pipes in the organ."

"What do you mean?"

"Well, it's off key when it plays."

"Sounds okay to me."

"You don't have much of an ear for music, do you?"

"I don't know, Slim. How do you figure that?"

"Can't ya hear that one note, every onc't in a while, when that pipe plays? It's flat."

"Never noticed it."

"That's cuz ya don't have a good ear for music. See, I can tell. I play the geetar ya know. Learnt it down in Texas when I was herd'n cattle down there. Plenty of time nights to fool aroun' and learn it. Learnt to play it pretty good. I got a good ear. I can tell that one pipe's got somep'n wrong with it. Mice must've chewed up somep'n in winter quarters. Plenty of mice in them barns."

"Well, I can't tell the difference. What are we going to do about it?"

"Well, nothin', I guess. If it don't bother ya, and most folks don't have a good ear like mine, so's I guess we can jist leave it. But I'll tell ya, every time I hear that sour note, it makes my skin crawl. I got such a good ear, ya know."

Shortly after that I fell asleep. Organ or no organ, I was out.

The organ created music as compressed air was blown through the perforations of a roll of paper music, activating certain pipes of the organ. Thus, the proper notes issued from the stately and highly decorated Wurlitzer, which with the accompaniment of its cymbals and drums created the music for a light-hearted and joyous occasion. The dozen or so rolls were played repeatedly over the season and even the years. In time you had heard them often enough that you came to know them pretty well.

I remember the spring of 1928. I was almost twelve years old. We opened and there was a brand new roll of music on the Merry-Go-Round. The tune it played, "Ramona," had been recently popular. I was familiar with it and delighted in humming and singing the song. The words were pure romance to me. I could just see "Ramona" with the "rambling rose in her hair," meeting her lover "by the Waterfall." He "blessed the day she taught him to care." My naive impression at my age of the beauty of their idyllic love was not disturbed when he admitted he "dreaded the dawn when he awoke to find her gone." I had yet to learn of that kind of love. I only knew that I felt sorry for him when she had to leave and spoil their romantic meeting "by the water-fall."

In spite of the fact that there was one note which was consistently flat on that old organ, "Ramona," still sounded good to me.

The Merry-Go-Round and a Ferris Wheel are pretty basic rides for a carnival. Carnivals are composed primarily of rides, shows, and concessions. Ours was a medium-sized outfit with eight rides, about ten shows most of the time, and about fifteen to twenty concessions. Circuses, in contrast, are essentially a performing arts type of entertainment, emphasizing difficult and often dangerous feats of physical skill, and with a special emphasis on trained animal acts. And of course, the clowns. It wouldn't be a circus without them.

During the period of time of our story, both types of outfits traveled from one spot to another, usually staying about a week, or whatever the traffic would bear. Circuses may contract the individual acts, generally under the auspices of the show's owner. Carnivals like this one, which was operated by my dad, Les Bodnar, may contract the individual rides, shows, and concessions, but most of the show, or even all of it, is generally operated by one principal owner. He is responsible for scheduling the show, and making all arrangements necessary for it to operate. It is not an easy task to coordinate all that is necessary for the success of such a large and varied organization.

Our carnival was known as the Calumet Amusement Company. We usually opened in the spring, close to Easter. The weather was often cool at that time of year. Many nights were downright cold and the midway would then be pretty empty. However, everything had been repaired and painted over the winter, and it was time to go. We would take a chance on the weather. Since our winter quarters were in

Crown Point, Indiana, we usually opened in nearby Gary. Another year, when the show winter-quartered in Riverdale, Illinois, we opened in Harvey, Illinois.

In Crown Point, the fairgrounds had several very substantial brick exhibit buildings which would house our wagons, the rides, the tents, and all that was part of the show, so the help could do their work indoors. Throughout the winter, equipment was repaired and maintained, trucks were overhauled, canvas was patched, and new wagons and shows were constructed. Almost everything received a new coat of paint or whatever was needed to decorate and add to the "flash."

Only a few workers were kept over the winter for this work. They were the more dependable and somewhat talented men in ways of mechanics, construction, painting, and decorating. They were a sober, hard-working, willing crew. I don't know how they came to be so loyal, maybe because some had no place to go for the winter, no homes and no money.

Even during the active season of the carnival, it was surprising that they remained steadily with us, considering how little they derived from the carnival life. It certainly was not glamorous and yet maybe it was rather adventuresome. There was no future in it for most of them. They were poorly paid and received no benefits other than for a small, year-end bonus. For some it was a second chance, escaping from whatever they fled: unhappy marriages, alimony payments, debts, and I suspect that a few were escaping from some criminal charge or a bad record somewhere. And for some it was a vagabond type of life which suited them. By and large they were young, footloose, fanciful, free of responsibilities, and without trades or special training. Most of them were not well educated; the only one I knew of with any degree of advanced education was our "Geek" of whom we shall speak later, who had two years at the University of Wisconsin, if we can believe him,

There was a general sense throughout the outfit that we were one. We operated as a unit, with a mutual feeling of interdependence. We relied on each other and we helped one another. This was especially true when we were on the road. We were amid strangers at those times with only the other members of the outfit to support us. We became a family.

At the end of each carnival season, those who had homes went home for the winter. Others went their various ways. Most of the workers probably bummed around, going to warmer climates. Gibtown in Florida was one of their usual winter-time haunts. They were a resilient group, familiar with the ways of the world and well aware of survival tactics. They knew how to work the system.

Those who had left for the winter pretty well knew when the show was to open in the spring. They would then show up, ready to go on the road. Some of our regulars came from Valparaiso, Gary, and Crown Point, Indiana. Others came from Pittsburgh, Madison, and other distant points but most came from Chicago. Some were respectable married men; others were seeking love on the fly, and some of them did manage to "score" fairly often, I learned.

I recall one early evening in a suburb of Chicago, we had just finished setting up and were getting ready to open. Al Beuse, who did much of our electrical work, was still in his work clothes after "cutting in" the concessions to the electrical cables leading from the transformer wagon when a little guy came on the lot carrying a rifle, dragging his daughter with him.

"Hey! You! You worka here?"

"Yeh," said Al."Whatsa matter?"

"I'm a lookin for'a Leetle Johnny. You knowa heem?"

"Why? Whatsa matter?"

"I'm a gonna fine that sonofabeech. Where he is?"

"I don't know." Said Al. "I haven't seen him around here."

"I gonna fine heem. I kill heem. Looka what he'sa do my sweet Rosa."

Al had already noticed the crying girl, with a face that was probably pretty at other times, but filled with terror at this time. She was only about five feet tall, but her figure, which now protruded grotesquely in the area of the lower abdomen, told Al the rest of the story. Just as there is said to be honor among thieves, it was part of Al's code to protect his co-worker. He had no idea where Little Johnny was.

"I gonna fine heem an he marry Rosa or I keel heem. Where he is?"

Well, this went back and forth for a while until the little guy was persuaded to put the gun in the toolbox of the transformer wagon while Al and others helped him look for Johnny. But they never found him. Johnny had taken it on the "lam" when he saw his fate approaching. The sheriff had been summoned, and when he arrived he cautioned the father to get his gun and take the girl home before he did something foolish. The old man was still railing about "dat leetle sonofabeech," still threatening to "get that Johnny" when he finally left the lot with Rosa, since it was obvious he was not about to find Johnny. Luckily, no one got shot, and probably equally for the best, no one got married.

We were familiar with Johnny's reputation. This neat, handsome little guy was a real Don Juan, but nothing like this had ever happened before.

He reappeared several nights later. My dad had heard about all that had occurred and that evening, after we closed, he had Johnny come over to the cookhouse. We didn't have an office wagon at that time. My dad usually sat at the corner table in the cookhouse where he had his frequent coffees and where he did most of his business.

As Johnny came over, my father beckoned him to sit down. "What was that all about, Johnny?" he asked.

"Gosh! I don't know," said Johnny.

"Come on now. You know what it's about, and I think I know what it's about. I wasn't born yesterday and I won't have you lying to me either."

"Well, I think that's the girl I met when we played Whiting last spring, and I gave her a free ride on the Ferris Wheel and we became good friends for that week."

"Yes?"

"Yeh, and we became very good friends. She liked me and I liked her too, a lot, but I haven't seen her since then."

"Go on."

"Well, I guess something happened to her, and her old man thinks I did it."

"Well, did you?"

"I don't know if I did or someone else did. You know how that goes."

"'No. Tell me."

"Well, some other guy could have done it to her too."

"And could you?"

"Yeh, but that doesn't mean I did that to her. We did some things a couple of times that week. Then when I told her I was looking for the right girl and would marry when I found her, I just couldn't keep her away. She had that loving personality. She never gave me a chance to explain that. Sure, I loved her in a certain way, but I didn't think she was the right girl for me. She never gave me a chance. I'd never marry her anyway."

"And why is that?"

"She was too experienced. I could tell right away. You know how you can tell how much they know. Besides, she told me she had made love before, but she said she had broken up with her old boyfriend and was feeling very lonesome. Maybe he got her that way. She said she wanted to get married. Well, I didn't, but I didn't want to spoil her fun by telling her that. You know how that is."

"Johnny, the fact remains that you could be the one."

"No. Honest, boss. Maybe it was some other guy."

"Either way, you should recognize that things like this can happen and have very serious consequences. The fellows who saw her on the lot say she may not even be eighteen years old. That could bring you a jail sentence."

"She said she was twenty one."

"Regardless, a young woman of that age is going to have a hard time finding a good husband to look after her and any child that she may have. That means a hard life for her and the kid as well. Isn't that right?"

"Yeh, I guess so."

"And did you think of that when you were having your fun with this young lady? If there is a child, you may have a responsibility toward it and the girl. From what I know of you, you are not likely to assume that. Your reputation for picking up with the ladies sounds like just a good time to you."

"Yeh, but they have a good time too."

"Maybe so, but you still have to think of all the other issues resulting from it; even the show, the carnival world, the guys you work with, they all come to be known as a bunch of bums because of things like this. It's time to take stock, my boy. Be a man. You're not a kid anymore."

"Yeh, I know."

"Think more seriously. Act responsibly. Think of the future."

"Yeh."

"And you had better start now. You may get away with things this time, but if you keep messing around, you'll find worse trouble along the way sooner or later. You understand?"

"Yeh, you're right. I know. I heard every word you said and I'm gonna straighten out. Honest, boss, believe me. You got it right and I know that. I'm gonna try. I don't want any more of this trouble. Honest. And thanks for telling me all this. I really appreciate it. No one else has ever talked serious to me like this or about anything else. Really. I appreciate it. Thanks, boss."

"OK. Now don't forget it. And if I hear anything more like this, you're gone. Got it?"

"Yep, I sure do."

"All right. Get back to the Ferris Wheel and help get those top seats off the Wheel for the night. We're expecting a storm. I don't want the Wheel to get blown over."

In the ensuing years, I thought more seriously about this. I hadn't really thought much about my dad and his attitudes in situations like this and others which developed in time, but I thought a lot about it over the years. I knew he was very strict about a lot of things, drinking, for example. He didn't approve of drinking. He had no use for drunks or even frequent use of liquor. He didn't approve of the immorality in which Little Johnny had indulged. He didn't gamble but here he was running a show with a lot of gambling concessions. I guess he thought it was okay to do so as part of his business, but he certainly did not allow himself to fall into that trap. He was very respectful of women. He showed love and kindness toward my mother, Julia, at all times. He recognized her too as a real helpmate in their work together with the carnival, and he accorded her due respect, especially in matters of finance and business. They were both hard workers, industrious, and ambitious, even to a fault. Further, my father was not afraid of hard, physical work. He was quick to lend a hand on moving nights if the situation demanded. He wasn't very religious. I know he believed in God, but he never went to church. However, over the years, I came to know many good people who were not particularly religious. There were many good points in his character, but in time I came to realize that his sense of values was indeed kaleidoscopic, with the mirrored and brilliantly colored stones contrasted by the occasional black or tarnished stones and empty spaces. Otherwise, how could he explain some of his actions in managing the carnival: the gambling, the dishonesty of some of the games of chance, putting in the "fix" with the police, and the exploitation of the "freaks" in the side shows, and of women in the "Girl Show"? These constituted the spurious values of the carnival business of that day. Even at my early age, I saw the error of these activities, and resolved to do better with my own life. I regretted seeing the loss of character, of integrity, and of honesty which abounded in that carnival world. My mother, fortunately, preached regularly against it, thereby helping to instill better principles of living into me. Her eight years of education in a Catholic school had more firmly instilled a better value system in her mind and mine.

But to get back to Johnny, he probably meant well at the time of the discussion with my dad, but I doubt that it did any good because several years later, after he had failed to show up that spring, he did show up at one of our spots, weak and rundown, talking of crazy things, and walking poorly because of difficulty in moving his legs. We were told he had syphilis. We learned some years later of his death.

There were also numerous show-people with the outfit, who did not fit this general description of the "help." These showmen and ladies were the owners and operators of some of the various rides, shows, and concessions constituting the outfit. They fit the category of ladies and gentlemen, a few of them of some means, solid citizens otherwise, who worked regularly at this occupation, and lived as family people do, raising and educating their children, looking after grandma, living in quiet neighborhoods or hotels, sometimes with other business ventures, for all the world like ordinary people, although in some cases it was a difficult stretch to rationalize the carnival life with their more genteel side.

Johnny Norman was the chief of his group of men who operated the gambling concessions with my dad. He lived with his wife, two sons, and his mother-in-law in the Hyde Park area of Chicago.

The Dennisons and their daughter, Eddytha, came from Cincinnati. They had a couple of concessions including the fishpond. On the road they lived in hotels or private homes

We, my mother and father and my sister, Mildred, two years younger than I, lived in a very modest home at the south end of Chicago, a nearly suburban area, a few blocks from the factories where my grandfather had worked, and a mile or so from the farm which my father had once worked for my grandfather.

Art Rexall owned two theatres in the suburban area of Chicago and lived in a posh North Side "near the lake" apartment, but in the summer he and his wife and Pekinese traveled with the show. They operated several concessions including a pitch-and-toss game. There for a small fee you received three wooden rings such as one uses for embroidery, which gave you the opportunity to try your skill at winning a valuable prize, apparently very easily. All you had to do was to toss and hook the ring securely over a wooden post four or five feet away, and you won the prize on that post, the glistening cigarette case, the Bowie knife, the German Luger or the Colt pistol or whatever was on that post. The guy behind the counter demonstrated how easily the ring slipped over the post. Not to worry. It was rarely necessary to replace one of those articles on the posts. The friendly people operating these games took very little chance of losing at the game. But if you wanted to take the chance that you could beat them at their game, they were happy to give you the opportunity.

In contrast, the guys at the working level, sometimes known as roustabouts with other outfits, lived in another world. Actually, we did not think of them as roustabouts. That too much suggests that they were bums. I never heard them referred to as anything but "the help." Some did live at home while we played the lots around Chicago, but when we were on the road, and when we hit the county fairs, theirs became a more gypsy-like life. A few at the more supervisory level could afford a cheap hotel. Most did not. Some lived in trailers, primitive compared to what we have today. Some lived in the enclosed carnival wagons. But mostly they lived in the concession and show tents with a cot, a few blankets, a suitcase, some extra clothing, and a few accessories for personal hygiene and cleanliness constituting their home on the road. They ate in the cookhouse which traveled with the outfit. Bathroom privileges were arranged for at some nearby home or gas station or other facility. Nature's more simple urgencies were relieved behind cover of canvas when it was more convenient to do so. They were an adaptable lot, and for them, life remained an adventure. They all had "Carnie" blood in their veins.

My dad first entered the carnival world working a part-time job on the Ferris Wheel at White City Amusement Park on the south side of Chicago, supplementing his income from the grocery business which he operated during the week. In time he wanted more of the carnival business, and so he and my Uncle Mike pooled their resources and bought a Ferris Wheel. That was in 1918.

Uncle Mike, whose last name was Sweedie, worked in the Ingersoll Factory but wanted something more in life. He was a smallish man, wiry, very genial, and married to my grandmother's niece, Aunt Theresa. That's how he got into the family. He gave up a good factory job when he entered the carnival world in which he became the part owner and ticket seller for the Wheel. After a few years, the unsteadiness of the carnival business unnerved him, so he went back to his factory job and its steady income. He sold his share in the Ferris Wheel to my dad.

At about that time, John DeJung came along with his Merry-Go-Round. He operated at street fairs and local celebrations. He wanted to operate full time with an outfit, so when he learned my dad was organizing a carnival, he joined up with my dad. They moved about, playing small celebrations for churches, small-town pageants, and similar events requiring the novelty of carnival rides to lend a spirit of fun to the occasion.

As it grew, the outfit acquired a few concessions, a popcorn wagon, a food concession, which also became the cookhouse, and later some games of chance like bingo or games of skill, requiring throwing or other actions; still later came the wheels of chance and other gambling games. In time, other rides and shows were added.

It was always interesting to see the show go up, to see a

city lot or fairgrounds, barren in the morning, transformed into the glittering flamboyant midway with a wide variety of entertainment for all by night. But it wasn't complete until the Merry-Go-Round, with its revolving lights and painted panels, its Arabians and thoroughbreds racing to the time-honored music of the organ, announced it as ready to go.

John DeJung's Merry-Go-Round was a beauty with its three-abreast rows of horses gliding up and down on their brass poles moving from a light trot to a gallop as the speed of the ride increased. A few zebras and donkeys and even a man-sized rooster were thrown in to give diversity to the more adventurous riders. Carousels had always been a major attraction with carnivals. They provided the color, the lights, the music, the illusion of horsemanship, and the dizzying motion which appealed to all ages. It was a rare child who resisted the impulse to mount a prancing steed, even a wooden one, with his Lippanzer-like gait, all under one's masterful control, while holding the reins attached to the rings of the bit in the horse's mouth, and with the safety of the brass pole in front of one to hang onto if the ride became too spirited. No fear of being kicked or bitten or thrown. The Merry-Go-Round and its organ, more than any other ride, created the ambience of the carnival.

John DeJung, who owned the Merry-Go-Round, was a stoic Dutchman, solid in his beliefs and loyalties, kindly and compassionate in his dealings with people. He had another interest with the show, Emma, the "Fat Lady." He looked after her. She lived with him and his wife Frieda. He brought her to the lot and took her home every night and brought her back the next day. He would help her up into the enclosed trailer which folded out on one side to make a platform to enlarge the viewing area, while she sat in her rocking chair in the central part of an enclosure at a slightly lower level. The area was furnished to resemble a comfortable home-like room. There she sat good naturedly, rocking comfortably, chatting with her viewers, knitting or reading, occasionally eating peanuts or a chocolate-covered cherry, displaying pounds and pounds of rolling flesh encased in a short-skirted, short-sleeved dress revealing her bountiful self. The banner in front proclaimed her at 600 pounds. I don't know, but at times when I looked at her, I wondered if that was her real weight or did she maybe knock off a few pounds to satisfy her vanity.

We had numerous other side shows over the years which featured a single attraction. Like Emma, they were presented in a fold-out type of trailer with one side opening half upward as a roof and half downward as a viewing platform, accessible by a set of stairs alongside the ticket box in front. The ticket seller was also the "grinder," with his steady spiel to entice the crowd to see the attraction. He was also the ticket taker. A generally efficient operation since the trailer, when folded up, also served to transport equipment when the show was on the move.

Some of these were "freak" shows as they were then called, which presented otherwise normal people with all the ambitions and hopes and passions of all of us, but for whom some quirk of development or choice made them different.

The "man who was born with the tail of a horse" was simply an extreme case of overgrowth of a residual of embryonic development. For many, however, the lecturer's explanation was more tenable, that the mother of our "freak" was frightened by a horse and that she put her hand to her back side at that moment, resulting in this curse visited on the gentleman.

This could be a a reasonable assumption to many of the

gullible of that day. They had accepted other similar expla-
nations in the past. In later years I encountered other ex-
amples of such ignorance.

I am reminded of the story told by the farmwoman who
rented a room to my wife and me at my last station in the
Army before going overseas in World War II. The farmer's
wife told of visiting her friend whose child had been "born
with the foot of a cow" after being frightened by a cow during her pregnancy. It sounded to me like a clubfoot, which
is indeed an unfortunate error in the development of a
human limb in-utero. My wife spent some time explaining
to our woman how these things really occur and that they
are not the result of a fright during pregnancy, at the end of
which time, our lady who had listened patiently to this explanation, stated matter of factly that however, in this case,
the friend really had been frightened by a cow. And that was
that! So much for science!

Some of these unusual presentations may be the result
of more devious causes.

My friend, "Butch" Butler of the Butler Amusements
Company, who owns one of the largest carnivals on the
road, tells of two sisters, twins, Mary and Madeline Ragan,
who were passed off as Siamese twins in a vaudeville act.
They had found a material, somewhat skin-like, of which
they had a garment made, joined at the waist to produce in-
stant Siamese twins, without the inconvenience of remain-
ing permanently joined as Siamese twins truly are.

A veteran showman, Ward Hall, told me of the two-
headed baby he displayed as part of one of his shows, usually
as the "blow-off" event. Initially he constructed it by removing the head of one doll and gluing it to another doll. The
juncture, covered by clothing, worked until Ward had a wax
two-headed doll made for the same purpose, even better.

"Butch" Butler also tells of the "duck woman," who tried out for a vaudeville act and was told by the "Siamese Twins" Ragans that she was too ugly for show business with her prominent teeth, recessed jaw, and frowsy hair. They told her she might have a chance if she had her teeth pulled and hair shaved. She returned a few days later with her head shaved and gums still bleeding slightly from having had her teeth pulled. Her face and mouth were swollen so she could utter only a quack-like sound. The twins were filled with re-morse. They felt they had to atone for this ill-conceived ad-vice to the poor lady. They seized on the idea of having a garment of feathers made to cover her head and body, and with her prominent nose, receding jaw, and quacking voice, they worked her into an act as "the duck lady," also known as "the quack-quack lady." It was some time later that the twins learned of the near demise of the "duck lady," who was now a feature in a carnival side show. Apparently view-ers of that show had indulged her fancy by throwing pop-corn to her, which she ate to the extent that she had convinced herself that popcorn was the right food for a duck, and that as a duck, that was to be her diet. It took some persuasion by a physician to convince her that she was not a duck and would have to change her diet.

One of our shows was "The Spider Lady," an illusion. Viewers walked into her parlor to find her in a recessed al-cove as a large, dark-bodied spider with hairy arms widely spread and moving slightly, with the pleasing face of a young woman atop the body of the spider. It didn't seem real. It aroused much speculation, but the barker assured the public that she had been born that way. I found out better in time. This was a very simple but clever illusion. The Spider Lady sat behind the scene, about eight feet square, which was composed of a downward angled upper panel with loosely attached spider arms and legs, which were reflected in a up-wardly angled mirror set to reflect the arms of the spider. The stuffed body of the spider superimposed on the mirror of the lower panel was topped by the head and face of a sweet young Spider Lady who looked at you through an opening at the point where the upper and lower panels met. Okay. You've paid your money; now you've seen the Spider Lady.

Other shows included "The Smallest Horse in the World," a miniature horse of the Argentinean Fallabella Breed of horses, bred to this small size, barely 28 to 34 inches high at the withers, with the body lines of a normal horse, not those of a pony.

There was the giant octopus. This was the real thing. But it did reek of the formaldehyde in which it was pre-served. Nevertheless, it gave one the rare opportunity to see this creature of the seas with massive body of mouth, eyes, and stomach, with radiating tentacles six feet long, the better to grasp you or anything else that came its way.

At times there would be a single, large and live snake as the featured attraction, a python or a boa constrictor. The handler was usually a rugged character from I know not whence, but who was seemingly comfortable in dragging these serpents from their warm places of rest, wrapping the snake with its powerful body over his neck and shoulders, while encouraging one to touch the shiny, scale-covered body, so that you would better understand how friendly these animals were.

However, the more usual snake show, one which we al-most always had with us, was housed in one of the side-show trailers. There was a canvassed pit inside a walled cubicle where visitors could peer over the top of the enclosure at a collection of ten or fifteen of these rascals, with the snake-charmer, sometimes a man and sometimes a woman, who was brave enough to mingle with them. There would be the usual small and colorful garden snakes, shiny blue racers, menacing black snakes, pretty corn snakes. so-called hoop snakes and whip snakes, and there always were rattlesnakes, all with their forked tongues lashing out, as they moved about. Once there was also a coral snake for a while – a beautiful thing, so poisonous and so small but cautiously kept in an aquarium-like glass enclosure. I never saw moccasins or cottonmouths. However, all the snakes we had were the real thing, live and dangerous to varying degrees, but I suspect the rattle snakes had been rendered safe in some way to avoid fatal accidents. I know these handlers were bitten from time to time; they proudly showed their scars, but I don't recall any one of them being bitten by a rattler. The diamond patterning on the backs of those rattlers was indeed a pretty sight, but that was enough. That was the extent of my interest.

Other shows were more extensive, sometimes having several attractions in one like the "House of 1000 Wonders." Others were exhibitions of doing and daring like the "Motordrome" with its cyclists riding on a vertical wall.

Not all of these shows were part of our organization. They may have contracted to show temporarily with us or with the association under which we were showing, such as the county fair associations.

Some of these shows would not be allowed today, such as one at the Lake County Fair in Crown Point one year. There, in a specially built trailer with one side open, but glassed-in, was a simulated hospital nursery. Spectators passed by on the viewing platform as they observed Siamese

Twins, infants, a few months old, who were carefully shown in their cribs or in the arms of an attendant, purportedly a nurse, complete with uniform and cap. These were really Siamese Twins, whose brief lives were being exploited. It was certainly interesting to view such a result of abnormal embryologic development, although it did not seem ethical to exploit them by such an exhibition. Such twins, joined at chest and abdomen as they were, rarely survived for very long at that time. I don't know the fate of these, since they were with the fair and did not travel with us.

At that same fair, at another time, there was an exhibit which made a life-long impression on me. It was probably done in cooperation with some health department. They presented a walk-through exhibition of a series of life-sized moulages depicting male and female human sexual organs infected with various venereal diseases. They looked mean and nasty. There was simulation of purulent gonorrheal discharges from male and female genitalia; angry, inflamed, ulcerated lesions which were labeled to be syphilitic chancres; chancroidal lesions; herpetic vesiculations; inguinal granulomatous growths; some dermatological conditions; and descriptions of the late effects of some of these diseases, such as the neurological conditions, locomotor ataxia (tabes dorsalis), paresis, etc. Oral as well as genital lesions were illustrated. This was enough to remember for a lifetime, warning one of the dangers of promiscuous or deviant sex.

Concessions were the final elements of the carnival. They were essentially either selling food or souvenirs, or providing opportunities to win prizes at games of skill or chance.

The "spots" at which we showed in the earlier part of the season were essentially in the Midwest, mostly around

Chicago and the industrial area of Northern Indiana, known as the Calumet area. That's why our carnival was known as the "Calumet Amusement Company." Later, in the summer and fall, we made a circuit of county fairs and celebrations in Wisconsin, Illinois, Indiana, and Michigan's Upper Peninsula.

When we made the fairs, it was most interesting to visit the exhibit halls and to see the animals, the 4-H efforts, the grandstand productions, the horse racing, the fireworks and all the spectacle associated with a county fair. This was rural America celebrating the year's work, showcasing the efforts of farm youth in their 4-H activities, stimulating competition in raising and producing the best in farm animals and produce. The carnival and its atmosphere added one more dimension for their enjoyment.

The carnival, as it evolved, became an extensive business. My dad, with his fourth-grade education, somehow developed the "moxie" to prosper in it. He was making what was considered a good, but not affluent, living in those days. However, his ambition to improve and enlarge the outfit to enable him to get the contracts for the better fairs and celebrations led to greater investments in equipment, with little left for personal comforts. My folks lived well, but frugally. My mother never did get the home in the select neighborhood she had envisioned and worked for. She had good business sense, and although she tried to curb some of my father's ambition for a larger and larger carnival, her efforts were rarely successful. Her education was also limited. In those days, few women had more than a high-school or grade-school education. My mother had finished the eighth grade and had taken a few business courses at night school, but the efforts of both my mother and dad, with their limited education and business expertise, were not really adequate for the great successes they envisioned. They did work hard at making the show a success.

Success required paying close attention to many details not seen as part of the world of entertainment. The circuit of "spots" where we were to show had to be arranged well in advance. Local arrangements had to be made for each location. Contracts for land rentals, provision for electrical services, facilities for the help, permits to operate, advance advertising and promotion, arrangements with trucking companies to augment our equipment in moving the show, and even arrangements with police departments were necessary to avoid conflicts between the law and gambling. Winter quarters and plans for the off-season were made. During the winter, the fair associations met and contracts with them for the next year were arranged.

My father did have help with the carnival as the outfit grew. He acquired Louie "the Jew" Berger as his advance agent. Louie's appellation as "the Jew" was given to distinguish him from the other Louies in the outfit. It was not a term of prejudice. It just happened to be the way people around the shows were identified. Some of these names equaled those of Damon Runyon's characters.

Louie helped with contacts and contracts for the fairs during the winter, planning for the next year. During the season, Louie would appear on the lot on the first day at the new location. He would talk business with my father and then spend the rest of the week at the next spot preparing for us, arranging for whatever business was unfinished that might be necessary to operate there. He had a good head for business and took a load of work off my dad. However, even Louie could not foresee all that lay ahead. Just as in any business adventure, and much of this was an adventure, there were pitfalls which were not regularly anticipated, and so in spite of the best attempts of Louie, my dad, and others, there were mishaps amid their successes, which resulted in dire consequences at times.

The carnival was year-round work, but since there was no income in the off-season my father had a second occupation by the only route available to him for the winter. As a farmer and later as butcher and grocery-shop owner, he learned the butchering of animals. He operated a small slaughter house during the winter, primarily for an ethnic trade. First generation Europeans often followed their traditions, having a hog slaughtered, storing their own meats, and preparing their own sausages. Slaughtering was strenuous work. The hours were long; it was exhausting work; but with his limited education and lack of other training or skills, my dad reverted to what he had learned as a boy on his father's farm. This was entrepreneurship at a basic level. He learned by experience, not the best way, but the only way available to him. This meant a certain amount of trial and error, which was costly at times.

However, on the whole, things went well that year, and as winter waned, we looked forward to spring with the usual anticipation of the opening of what we hoped would be a successful season.

1928, The Year We Opened in Gary

IT WAS EASTER SUNDAY OF 1928, ONE OF THE YEARS IN which we opened in Gary. It was spring and still very cool at night. My folks had taken me and my sister Millie to the lot with them. It was exciting to learn of the changes which had been made over the winter, to see the glitter and "flash" of the entire oufit, to see old friends, and to experience, with everyone else, the annual hope that this was the start of a banner year for the carnival.

It was grand to see it in operation again. Everything was sparkling clean and fresh. The rides had been newly painted. Even the Merry-Go-Round horses, had been renovated by an itinerant artist who worked over the winter for John DeJung. Every light socket had a bulb lit in it, brightening the night. Several of the shows had new banners for the new acts, namely the Ten-in-One which was to be operated by new show-people, the Conroys.

The usual members of our carnival "family" were there: the Pettits, the Normans, Mr. Haywood, Charlie Peterson, Mr. and Mrs. Dennison, the Rexalls, and the returning and reliable help – the regulars who worked the outfit.

Our entire Bodnar family was also there that evening, to see the splendor of the show. That included my dad's two brothers, Uncle Henry and Uncle Louie, and their families. Both uncles had an interest in the outfit. At one time it was known as the "Bodnar Brothers Show."

Uncle Henry was a little older than my dad, and just a little taller. He was strong and well built. He had farmed grandpa's farm after grandpa died. He had bought a ride, the Chair-O-Plane, when he sold grandpa's farm to join my dad. He was really an outdoorsman and loved hunting. Many a gunshot I found with my teeth when I ate the rabbits and pheasants he gave us, He had a loud raucous laugh that bothered me, when he learned of something funny that we had done. He and my father were very competitive with each other. This especially showed in the baseball games they occasionally organized at the lot, each one captaining his group of "Carnies."

Aunt Susie, his wife, was a large woman, rather bossy and demanding, proud of her parentage, and quick to find fault in others. She did not come out to the lot very often, and she didn't let her daughters come very often either. She or her older daughter sold tickets for the Chair-O-Plane when they did come. Three of my cousins were their children.

Henry, their son, was just six weeks older than I. He was built sturdier than I was. I guess you would say I was more "wiry." Henry was very smart in school and did well in almost everything including sports and music. We were competitive, in spite of his physical advantage. We did a lot of things together. We were good buddies.

His sister, Esther, two years younger, was a pretty, sweet, cherubic little girl. She and Millie were good friends.

Charlotte, his other sister, was two years older. She ws rather aloof, and very very smart. She was first in our class of 150 at Fenger High School in Chicago. Henry was second, I was fourth, and our cousin Irene was seventh.

Uncle Louie was a little younger than my dad, a little shorter and quite thin. It was fun to be with him. He was always jokng around, not the serious type. We kids really liked him.

His wife, Aunt Marie, was sister to Aunt Susie, but was shorter and fatter. She was quiet, good natured, and was accepting of a life which was not as satisfying as her sister's due to Uncle Louie's peccadillos – he might go on a "toot" almost any time and be gone for days.

Their children, Irene and Carrie, were close to my age, Irene a little older, and Carrie younger – both good cheerful friends and cousins.

I had mentioned that Aunt Susie was a "proud" woman' She was quick to make a point at times that her father was a superintendent at the steel mills and my mother's father was only a furnace stoker for the "coke ovens" at the gas plant in the South Chicago area – one upsmanship!-and at that level.

We cousins had a good time together that opening night. We did all the rides. We saw the new shows. We bought popcorn from Art Pettit and hamburgers at the cookhouse. In the background was the buoyant music of the Merry-Go-Round organ and its occasional wheeze. We had a good night of it.

I was eager to see one of our new shows in action. During the winter at Crown Point we had built a Motordrome. I had been given a hammer and nails and helped in the construction of it.

The year before, we had visited the largest carnival of that time, the Johnny J. Jones Exhibition Shows, which was playing in Chicago Heights. I had gone with my dad and some of his henchmen to see the Motordrome with that outfit. It had been decided that this was a great attraction for the show and we were to have one. The trip was to get ideas for the dimensions and construction of this circular structure with vertical walls, somewhat like a silo. The walls were bound together with nuts, bolts, and cables within which daredevil motorcycle riders ran their machines, spinning around the interior at nearly a right angle to the wall, held there by centrifugal forces, performing fearless devil-may-care maneuvers on their motorcycles.

It was a thrilling show. The twenty-four-foot walls were surrounded near the top by a platform for the spectators. A cable guard-rail extended inward over the wall to prevent the machines from hurtling over the wall and to protect the spectators. This was overall topped by colorful canvas. New banners had been made, with the artist depicting these stunt riders hanging precipitously against the wall and proclaiming them to be the greatest in the world. "The Wall of Death" said the banners. These towered over the platform on which the bally was held.

Looking into the arena, some 60 feet wide, one saw two vintage Indian motorcycles of a type adaptable for this type of activity. There was another of these on the bally platform that was used to attract the attention of the crowd by running it on its stand, full throttle, its roaring punctuated by interval staccato bursts, creating enough noise to stop you in your tracks to learn what this was all about.

The main rider and manager of the Motordrome was also the front-talker. Bob Mercer was a seasoned, stoop-shouldered veteran of cycling, his face deeply scarred in several areas, which, with his slight limp, credentialed his courage on wheels despite what must have been numerous frightful occasions. His wife, Wanda, was the other rider, although we were never sure they were really married. She was a physically attractive, good-looking woman, despite a slight scar on one cheek. She had a large head of flaming red hair, and she was, as the Carnies described her, well built.

I was too young at the time to appreciate what a well-built woman was, but I gathered it referred to the fact that the individual was no longer flat across the chest like a boy, but was now definitely a woman. And the less flat and more expansive the chest area, the better built was she. Anyway, Wanda was definitely well built.

When they were ready to put on a show, after several appearances on the bally with Wanda blasting away on the motorcycle and Bob hawking the show, and after they had at least a fair-sized tip, they entered the Motordrome through a panel which was closed behind them to complete the bowl-like arena. It took a few minutes to warm up their wheels, making certain to again blast away to lure a few more in for the show and to create a sense of excitement in the crowd.

Then Bob took the first spin, quickly running his machine counter-clockwise as we looked down into the bowl. He took a preliminary round about the inclined base of the bowl and then he was on the wall. He seemed at ease; then he revved it, and with a few bursts, the machine began to roar and spin, hanging onto the vertical walls like a fly seeking an exit through the window. A half dozen of these turns and he was back down.

At that point, Wanda revved up her machine and took off. She did the same maneuvers that Bob had done. She showed her courage with aplomb.

After she came down, Bob went up and performed a more daring maneuver, diving up and down the wall as he circled it, coming too close to the guard rail for my comfort whenever I watched the show.

Now it was Wanda's turn and she went up doing the same maneuvers but somewhat less daring in her dips and dives.

Meanwhile, Bob revved his machine again, and now they were both on the walls racing each other as Wanda slowed and Bob passed her and she, in turn, passed him. A few rounds of this and then they took a break. A few puffs on a cigarette and Bob was ready to go again.

This time it was "Look, ma, no hands." That's what he did. Before we knew it he had taken his hands off the handlebars and after a few of such turns he had the motorcycle gently dipping up and down somewhat as he had done earlier. Man, that took nerve.

In the finale, they were both dipping up and down, avoiding each other yet performing a symmetrical dance-like movement, again proving their mettle. They put on these risky shows several times a night. That was "show biz." That was their life.

After the show, Bob puffed on a cigarette while he and Wanda talked to Al Beuse, who had been taking tickets for the show. Al had a lot of questions for them. When he asked what shows they had been with, Bob explained: "We were with the Johnny Jones Shows. I was second rider, but I wasn't getting along with the top rider, so I was glad to make the change when I had a chance to come to this outfit."

"And how about you?" Al asked of Wanda.

"Oh, I was just a little homebody," she said, "hopping an occasional ride, riding 'bitch' behind some guy or other until Bob came along and taught me to ride. Actually, I had learned to ride with the guys by then. I didn't like riding the pillion seat and wanted to ride my own 'wheel.' I was crazy about riding, but when I took in Bob's shows a few times and he offered to teach me to climb the wall, that was it for me. It's wild. I love it."

She was giving Al some kind of a penetrating look as she said the last few words. "I'm sure you're good at it," said Al. There was a dead silence as Bob looked at one and then the other of them. Bob told Wanda to get ready for the next show. Al wandered away to talk to the ticket seller. I learned all this as Al told it to my dad when we all went to a ballgame together one afternoon.

Al was my dad's right hand man. He wore many hats in the outfit. He was sort of a supervisor, gofer, bodyguard, and buddy. I guess you could say he was a pretty good-looking guy, about six feet tall and well built, a smooth talker and a good dresser, always in suit, tie, and Panama hat when not doing physical labor. He did all kinds of jobs around the show, fitting in wherever needed and had no specific assignment otherwise that I could see. He even lived in our home in a basement apartment that we had fixed up for him. He also worked with my dad's other business, slaughtering hogs in the winter.

On the carnival moves, Al drove the Fordson tractor, spotting the trailers for loading and unloading the rides and shows. Setting up, he did a lot of the electrical wiring from our transformer wagon to the individual boxes. I remember him being the barker at one time for the "girl show" and another time for the "fun house." Once he subbed for the clown in the high-diving act, after the clown was hurt. Al dressed up on that occasion as the clown, stepping off a platform thirty-five to forty feet in the air, legs cycling as if trying to get back up to the platform as he dropped into the tank of water below.

He was a good all-around man. Apparently he was even better as a ladies' man. This became evident later in the year when Wanda showed up with a black eye, the result of a disciplinary move by Bob Mercer when he learned of some shenanigans between Wanda and Al. She left Bob and the show not too long thereafter. Bob found a young guy to do her job, but the show didn't seem to attract people as well as when Wanda was there.

There was another first that year. We bought a "Lindy Loop." It was a new ride named after America's hero of 1927, Charles Lindbergh, who had flown the Atlantic solo except for a cat as company. The passengers on this ride rode in a shell-like carriage on wheels, cradled on two semi-circular arms. These cradles were connected as a series, propelled by arms sweeping from a central hub to an undulating circular track, about 40 feet wide. As the ride progressed, the shell rocked back and forth in the cradle of arms and with the undulating track on which it rode, it created a thrilling, out-of-control, "let me out of here" sensation. As the ride moved faster and faster, the screams of the patrons were enough to attract other adventurous souls longing for that experience. The ride was popular enough so that the cost of admission was higher than the other rides. It was 15 cents rather than just the ten cents for the other rides.

Another one of my dad's "right-hand" men was "Blackie." He was boss on the Lindy Loop; his co-worker was "Farmer." Blackie also did the spotting of trailers on the moves and the electrical wiring for the show, just as Al and Dago Louie did. Blackie was white but with a really dark skin so he was almost black, one of those dark Sicilian types. But he was a good guy, quiet, honest, conscientious, and dependable. He was divorced but sent his ex-wife money regularly and bragged about his teen-age son, who was doing so well academically and involved in sports in high school. The boy lived with his mother. Outside of that bit of pleasure in his life, Blackie seemed rather withdrawn and depressed. He missed his family.

At that time we had the Lindy Loop and six other rides, the Chair-O-Plane, the Whip, the Tilt-A-Whirl, a Kiddie Airplane Ride, and the usual Merry-Go-Round and Ferris Wheel. In fact, for a time we were joined by another Ferris Wheel owner, and we had two Wheels running side by side.

A few years earlier, my dad had sold a share in the Wheel to Uncle Louie to help finance the purchase of the Whip. However, Uncle Louie, as I inferred earlier, was a very outgoing guy, a real happy-go-lucky, good-time kind of guy, poor at work and business, but good at partying. When Uncle Louie failed to make a go of it, the Wheel reverted to my dad. Uncle Louie continued with the outfit as boss of the Ferris Wheel.

The Whip was the wild ride of those earlier years. The seats were in a round half tub-like arrangement on wheels, attached to spring-loaded arms, which were attached in turn to a cable that moved the tubs around an oval steel-platformed course. The cable, to which the arm of the tub was attached, wound around the interior of the oval track, and was moved along by 25-foot-wide turntables at each end of the central platform with one of these turntables being attached by gears to the motor on the central platform. As the ride moved about the ends of the oval, a "crack the whip" force spun the tubs widely, and as they returned to the straightaway platforms, the spring loaded arms gave a further whip and snap to the riders hanging firmly onto the handlebars, either praying or screaming for their lives.

During those years when the Whip was our best ride, it was also more or less the business center for the outfit. My mother sold tickets, and in the evening when the carnival closed, the other rides, shows, and concessions checked in to her, each with their proceeds in individual money bags, to be counted at home the next morning. It was understood that a number of the work force hang around the ticket box at these times to act as a deterrent to any potential robbery. The help drew what money they needed from day to day, but my mother was stingy with them. She knew their ways and that by season's end, they would be penniless unles she limited their withdrawals against their earnings. It was usually a rather fun time, the guys standing around, joshing, gossiping and joking, and trying to cajole my mother into increasing their allotment.

One of the characters working the Whip at that time was a cheerful, very dark, shiny-skinned Negro named "Shine." As the talk went on after hours, he would come out onto the area where riders stood on an elevated platform waiting their turn for a ride. This became a stage for Shine to tap-dance for us. He would start out with a few soft slow steps, and as he drew attention, he would get into some fancier moves, with fast staccato steps, bouncing into his up-and-down movements, his feet nimbly beating out their rhythmic message. It didn't take long for me to get taps put onto my shoes so I could work at the steps he showed me. He was popular with all of us. He was married, from Gary, and lived with his family. He was a solid worker. He had trouble finding other work because he had a prison record. He had stolen a car as a young man.

"Why did you do that?" I asked him one day.

"Oh, I was a crazy young guy then," he said." I hung around the corners a lot with the other guys. We had nothin' else to do but think of things we would like to do, so one day a couple of us decided we wanted to take a trip to Chicago."

"And you stole a car to go to Chicago?"

"No. Not me. One of the guys hangin' out with us knew how to wire a car to start it without a key. He knew where a car was parked all day behind a furniture store over on Broadway by a guy who worked there. He said it was an easy car to wire. So he went over there and pretty soon he showed up with the car."

"But he stole the car. You didn't, did you?"

"Nope, but what happened, we went to Chi and went to a club where the other guys got to partying and when we decided to go home, I was the only one sober enough to drive. I might have been okay but the police were already on the lookout for us, and when we got to Gary, they spotted us and arrested us. They got me for driving the stolen car. I went to jail for that.

"It cost me a good job I had at the 'mills' and I almost lost the wonderful girl friend I had. That was a hard way to learn a lesson. It's made a big difference in my life."

I was sure glad to know he was married now and had straightened out his life. We did not regard him as a criminal in any way.

Another guy, one who had difficulty finding other work, was a deaf mute. He was only about thirty-five years old but he looked sixty. He was one of the most cheerful and like-able guys in the world, in spite of his lack of speech. Actually, his hearing was okay. He just didn't have the gift of speech. In later years I thought it was pretty mean that he should have been given his nickname, but he was not known generally by any other name than "Dumbie." It was not said out of meanness, and it didn't refer to his intellect which, of course, was normal. Neither did he seem to resent it. He accepted the fact that he was speechless, so-called "dumb," and so what? "Make of life what it is," must have been his motto as he went through it day by day with crude gestures and grunts for language. You had to love a guy like that. He ran the Whip.

Dago Louie was always there too. These names were not derogatory, just a means of personal identification. He was Italian and of a very swarthy appearance, giving one the impression that the Mafia could be just around the corner. He also was married and had kids. I never heard that he had been in trouble. He seemed perfectly okay with us and should have been able to do better with his life, but his swarthy appearance and lack of education or skills must have been great disadvantages to him. He lived on the South Side around 55th Street. We frequently picked him up on our way to the lot while we were playing spots west of Chicago. He was boss on the Whip and also did a lot of the electrical hookups and other jobs around the outfit, another all-around man.

The other rides we had at the time included the Chair-O-Plane, which Uncle Henry owned, and the Tilt-A-Whirl, owned by Mr. Haywood. We had a ride for a few months at one time in which people sat in seaplanes as they flew around in a circle some thirty feet off the ground, but my dad sold it after a scary accident. The connector to one of the four chains holding a seaplane broke at its welding as the ride was flying through the air, dropping one corner of the body of the seaplane dangerously. No one was hurt but there was no need to trust the ride further since it might have other structural weaknesses.

There was also a "kiddie-ride" for children. There were five little airplanes, each of which seated two children and whirled them around in a circle a few feet off the ground. This ride had been purchased with the intention that all proceeds from it were to go toward my college education. That was already one of our dreams at the time. The die was cast. I was expected to go to college.

I did not know the owner of the Tilt-A-Whirl very well, but I knew his son, who was about my age, who came to the carnival once in a while. Jerry Haywood was a year behind me in school in Chicago. We were friends and pals when he came. Usually we would go on some of the rides and watch Bob Mercer in the Motordrome, but mostly he liked to go into Jackie Coyle's "House of 1000 Wonders."

Jackie was a small, hunch-backed, grumpy little old guy who owned this show. He and his sister, Erma, lived together in the same enclosed trailer which transported his stuff. She looked after him, cooking their meals in the trailer in which they lived frugally. She sold tickets for the show. They didn't do much in the way of promoting their show. They left it to a series of banners to promote it. There were banners picturing grave-robbing armadillos; fierce Indians fighting against white settlers; Yankee Generals in full dress uniform leading their men into battle in the Civil War and the Mexican War; helmeted troops in the trenches in World War II; cave men squatting around a fire; and one banner picturing wolves, lions, tigers, and a mean-looking eagle, eying an infant in a basket in the woods, all of which was apparently relative to the wonders to be found inside the tent for one thin dime. And it was true.

Jackie had somehow amassed an eclectic collection of artifacts, antiquities, stuffed animals, uniforms of the various armies pictured, a variety of firearms of those various eras, and a lot of Indian articles. Most of these were displayed in dusty cases covered with chicken wire to keep out hands which might seek to appropriate these articles. There were mannequins wearing soldierly uniforms and Indian dress; cases of arrows and spears; arrow and spear heads; old broken pottery; primitive tools of early man; and glassy-eyed, stuffed, and slightly moth-eaten badgers, eagles, cougars, and other wild animals. Only the hard-shelled armadillo was intact. It was spooky, and Jackie roamed the aisles between exhibits warning any suspicious youngster to "keep your hands off" in a high-pitched voice.

Jerry found all of this extremely interesting. It was okay, but I was somewhat scared by Jackie and the rather grim and sinister appearance of all that stuff, so I didn't go in there much unless Jerry was around.

At other times we might go over to the "Ten in One." This show was in a long tent with a row of banners in front showing the tattooed man (he really was, from toes to the neck); the fire eater (he did tricks like juggling burning brands or squirting a liquid from his mouth across a fire to produce a big flame); a contortionist (she could walk on her hands with her legs tucked behind her head); the guy who could walk on broken glass and hot coals; the sword swallower, (he could tilt his head back and work a small sword down his throat); the girl who was turning into stone (actually she was born with a condition in which bone was forming in her muscles); the smallest person in the world (she was born with a condition resulting in so many fractures that she never did grow normally); a giant (he was really big, like Frankenstein, because of some gland overworking); and the glass blower who made flowers and things you could buy. It wasn't until years later, in medical school, that I learned the real cause of the abnormal medical conditions which these people presented.

Sometimes there were other acts, such as when the Conroys were with the show in 1928. Their teen-age sons were called Dempsey and Tunney, and they boxed each other for three short rounds as one of the featured acts. Their sister was the contortionist. Their mother sold tickets, and their dad was the "frontspeaker" on the "bally." He ran the show. The same fellow who swallowed swords was also the fire eater, tattooed man, and walked on glass and coals.

Dempsey was my age, and we tried to get him to do things with us, but he could only do so between times when he boxed his brother. Tunney was older and a better fighter, and sometimes Dempsey would get hurt in their bouts. Then Dempsey would get angry and really go after his brother. These bouts, although faked as real, did carry over with bad feelings between the brothers at times.

Uncle Henry owned the Chair-O-Plane as well as the shooting gallery and the "Striker." On the Chair-O-Plane, you were in bucket seats suspended by long chains from the circular top of the ride, As the top turned, it spun you out into the air at about a thirty-degree angle about thirty feet above the ground. This was a popular ride. My cousin, Henry, sometimes sold tickets for it, but usually he and I were free to do as we pleased. We frequently tried our hand with the "Striker."

Here you took a hefty swing with a long wooden mallet, about three feet long, striking the rubber pad on a lever arm. The other end of the lever then caused a weight on a rail to shoot up the backboard, to a height depending on the power of your hit. It went up about twenty feet and if you did that it struck a bell and you won a prize, a cigar, or a box of chocolate-covered cherries. My cousin, Henry, could get it up about twelve feet. I could only make eleven. But he was bigger than I was.

We were occasionally allowed to shoot a sleeve of bullets a t the "Shooting Gallery." This was a steel-walled concession because real guns and ammunition were used, twenty-two caliber rifles. The bullets were twenty-two "shorts." We shot at bull's-eye targets and at stationary and moving steel targets in the shapes of squirrels and rabbits. Henry's dad didn't allow us to do that often because of the cost of bullets.

Henry and I were really good friends. He made the county fairs with his dad. Our favorite pastime during the days at fairs was to find a place to swim. At Crown Point we swam in the lake in the center of the racetrack. In Portage, Wisconsin, we swam in the Wisconsin River. In Menominee, Wisconsin, we rented a boat all day, and fooled around the weed-filled lake, swimming in the open and deeper water in the middle of this small lake.

We were in the same class in school, and so we did a lot there too. Henry was only a little older than I; he also seemed to be a little better than I was at almost everything. Because his dad owned the "Shooting Gallery," he shot more often than I did, so in school he made the rifle team in ROTC and I didn't. He outranked me in school, was a better swimmer, and even played the violin better. However, I was a better batter and a faster runner than Henry, who was actually a little bit fat. So I had him on that.

There were other families around the show with kids. The Pettits ran the cookhouse. Mr. Pettit did the cooking. Mrs. Pettit waited on the counter or the few tables in the back. Their older son Tom ran the griddle and their other son, Art, worked the popcorn wagon. Art was a jolly, fat, redheaded kid. I can still hear him barking "Pea corn hot nuts chew can and gumdy."

Art and Tom were always working so we didn't do much

together, but on cold evenings I would sit in the popcorn wagon with Art. It was nice and warm in there.

The Dickinsons ran the penny pitch concession. You threw pennies on a board with copper wires and if the penny landed across the wires, a light went on and you won a prize. Their son, Jack, was a few years older than I, and so he had to work all the time. His sister, Norma, was about my age. About all I can remember about her was when we played a spot in Indiana. I think it was Muncie. It was some kind of a week-long street celebration and my dad took me along. My mother didn't go. There was nothing to do during the day but my dad would take me to the lot to do whatever he had to do, and the Carnies would look after me. I remember one day when Norma and I were playing, and one of the things we did was to go into Charlie Peterson's wrestling show.

Charlie was an old-time wrestler with cauliflower ears and a coarse voice, but he was a kind man. He had our family to his place at Lake Geneva one year, and I had the worst sunburn ever after being out on his lake all day.

His show was about wrestling. Charlie would bring his wrestler out on the bally platform and after a lot of ear-shattering clanging of steel brake drums and a lot of "Hi –Look, come over." Charlie would talk of his great fighter and his wonderful exploits, further announcing that his fighter was willing to take on all comers if there were any real red-blooded he-men in that town. A purse was offered to any man brave enough to take on Charlie's wrestler, and an even greater prize if the brave man won. There was invariably someone in the crowd who considered himself a great wrestler and was willing to enter the ring for the pride of the community and some prize money. The willing spectator always seemed to be from some country town nearby. I also remember seeing the same guy at several different lots and fairs.

With the proper exhortations, Charlie would pretty well fill the tent with townies eager to see Charlie's great wrestler get his ears knocked off by their local champion. If that local champion won, as he so often did, a return match was challenged for an even bigger crowd the next evening, and of course, if he were beaten, the deciding match would be held the third day. Charlie refereed the matches, and they were great exhibitions, not as flagrant as today's matches for TV, but still a good show.

Anyway, Norma and I went in there, and she wanted to wrestle and, of course, I knew I could easily beat a girl, and so we did. We got up on the padded ring, starting from our appropriate corners, advancing, arms spread, and crouching in good wrestling form, grappling falling, squirming, putting arm locks, toe locks, half Nelsons, and a lot of body holds on each other. In time I came to realize that there is a lot of use of the body in wrestling because either I would find myself face up with her on top or she managed to get under me, her face up to mine. After we had called a break, she decided she had to "go." She could "go" under the wrestling platform but instead she chose to "go" in the area where the sidewalls of the tent overlapped. I guess you could say she propositioned me when she offered to show me hers if I showed her mine. When I refused she squatted down and "did it" anyway. I had to turn away quickly so I would not be obligated to show mine. The Dickinsons were only with us a few weeks as they had other places to go, but I sure remember Norma.

Young Johnnie Norman was maybe a year older than I. His duties with the stock wagon were not very restrictive so we did a lot together. He told some wild stories of the girls in his part of the city: parties when parents were gone, spinning the bottle, going into bedrooms to kiss and stuff that I didn't really believe. His dad ran the gambling joints for my dad. Mr. Norman had a funny voice, very deep and rasping. He always made you feel good by asking about school and things like that. He had a group of men with whom he had worked at various places over the years operating gambling concessions. Behind their backs, they were known as Jackie Norman and his Forty thieves.

Johnnie's brother, Charlie, was older and was a "stick," also known as a "shill," for their concessions. His mother and even his grandmother also "shilled" for their concessions when they came to the lot. Johnnie's mother always had her big Chow with her. He was the first animal I had seen with a purple tongue. He wasn't too friendly, and although I liked to pet dogs, I didn't bother with him too much. When Charlie and his mother and his grandmother "shilled," they would play at one of the wheels or other games. They would appear to be part of the regular crowd attending the carnival and playing at one or the other of their concessions. This encouraged other people to play. Of course, they soon won, thereby further enticing others to play. They would appear to have won the prize legitimately and walk around the midway with it in front of the other concessions to show that anyone could win at those games of chance. Eventually they would return the prize to the stock wagon. Some of the prizes were too big for the ladies to carry, and so Charlie would win those. Those were the bicycles or child-sized automobiles, the kind you had to pedal. Sometimes the games were for prizes like hams, or a basket of groceries, or baskets of fruit. The smaller prizes were kewpie dolls, boxes of candy, stuffed animals, blankets, funny colored glassware and vases, Japanese tea sets, lamps, and clocks, and stuff like that.

We weren't to talk to any of the "shills" when there might

be a "mark" around. I remember once going up to Rose, who was Kiki Tyler's wife. She was shilling for him when I walked up and asked her if she was going to win something as she always did. I didn't know it but some guy had walked up near me and looked as if he might be interested in playing. I heard Kiki say in a soft firm tone of voice "ixnay ackincray." I got it. I didn't say another word. I just walked away.

Pig Latin was a convenient tongue, and Kiki had just told me "nix cracking" which meant "no wise cracks" or something like that. He didn't want the "mark" to suspect that Rose was a "stick."

Henry and I had another more complicated form of language too. "Eaz" was implanted after the first letter of each word. For example, "go home" would be "geazo heazome." A lot of people could understand Pig Latin but not the complicated one we could use.

When the other kids were around and if they had no jobs to do, we wandered around the lot at night going on the rides or check to see what was new in the shows, or we might go through the funhouse again, or to the penny arcade. We'd get a hamburger at the cookhouse or maybe a Coke. If there were no other kids around, I might sell tickets for one of the rides or shows for a while, or my sister, Millie, and I might do some of those things or maybe go over and talk to Eddytha.

Eddytha was the daughter of Mrs. Dennison, who ran the fishpond. Eddytha helped in their joint. Mrs. Dennison was a very nice-looking lady. She dressed well and was somewhat formal and quiet. She didn't let Eddytha spend much time away from her unless my sister was with us. Eddytha always had to get her mother's permission to do things with us and had to tell her mother what we were going to do and how long we would be gone. Mr. Dennison looked more like a banker or a business man. He was always well dressed in suit and tie. He was a big man with something of a belly. "A very smooth operator," my mother said.

Mr. Dennison was not Eddytha's real father. Her real father was Greek and had a nice restaurant in Cincinnati. Eddytha's mother had worked as cashier in the restaurant. That's where Mr. Dennison met Eddytha's mother. Eddytha was about five years old when Mr. Dennison came to the restaurant. He and Mrs. Dennison fell in love, and so she divorced Eddytha's real father and married Mr. Dennison. She took Eddytha with her. Mr. and Mrs. Dennison had only been married for seven years. He treated Eddytha as their child.

During most of the year, Eddytha went to a Catholic boarding school in Cincinnati and was around the show only in summer or during spring vacations. The rest of the time her Greek father looked after her and paid for her to attend that boarding school. She told me, that year when we opened in Gary, that the next year she would attend the school's Academy. She was in the same grade as I, so I guess the academy was like a high school. She was really nice. Pretty in a tall, stately manner, smooth skinned – "olive skinned," my mother said. Eddytha had very good manners and talked nicely but she had a peculiarly low voice for a girl. It may have been from hollering while she helped in her mother's concession, calling to people to give them a free chance at the fishpond. If they did take a free chance, they found that they would have won a good prize. However, their luck usually ran out pretty quickly if they paid and took a chance.

Eddytha let us fish, and when we caught one of these little wooden fishes floating by in the current of the trough across the front of the joint, she showed us what we would have won. She showed us the number on the tab at the fish's mouth, which corresponded with the number of the prize. If it was a large number, over a hundred, you won a good prize, like a lava lamp, or a box of candy, or some carnival glass, or maybe even a Japanese tea set. But if the number was smaller, you only won something like a Chinese finger trap, or a paper horn to make noise with, or one of those things you blow out like a snake. Eddytha showed us how she could handle the tab in the fish's mouth in one way or another to have it show a larger or smaller number. People always got fish with small numbers unless they fished several times, and then Eddytha's mother would "throw a cop" to that person, meaning she saw to it that they won a good prize.

Mr. Dennison was very nice to Eddytha. She liked him. He didn't seem to work much, although he did help tear down and put up his concessions when we moved. Mostly he hung around with my dad or Mr. Norman, drinking coffee in the cookhouse, or he checked on his other concessions. The "Big Six" wheel was his, and the "Cat Rack," and the "Scales," to guess your weight.

The Cat Rack was a "flat" joint. That is what the Carnies called concessions that had a gimmick. You paid for so many balls which you threw at these stuffed cats on a shelf. You had to knock these fuzzy fringed cats off the rack. You could knock them off if you hit them right, but you could only knock them over and not down when the "gimmick" was on. And so you couldn't win when the operator pushed a lever which pushed back a second shelf behind the cats so they would not fall off the rack.

The Big Six wheel was legitimate, no gimmick. It was a beautiful wheel, four to five feet in diameter, white enameled with painted, black figures of various combinations of dice at all the slots around the wheel. The layout on the counter was much like those in any casino but a winner was decided with each turn of the wheel. This was a "percentage wheel." There were a lot of odds against the player. Mr. Carsons, who had worked in some big casinos when he was younger, ran it. People who liked to "shoot dice" were really attracted to this.

The Scales were also honest. It was just that "Whitey," who ran the concession for Mr. Dennison, was so good at guessing people's weight that he didn't lose too often. Even if he did miss by more than three pounds either way, which he was allowed, the prize was a box of chocolate covered cherries, which were not too expensive anyway. But Whitey won most of the time. Sometime he had to poke and feel how well some people were muscled to get it right. He especially had trouble guessing women's weight and often had to poke around a lot before he got it right. Some women would laugh and scream ad push him away when he did that and didn't give him a fair chance to get it right.

The Dennisons were nice people; there were others with the outfit.

The Rexalls were nice, but they didn't have any children They owned two theatres in one of the suburbs of Chicago with Mr. Rexall's brother, but Mr. Rexall liked the carnival business, and so he and Mrs. Rexall and their Pekinese dog were Carnies during the season.

They had a concession that was very special. It was a pitch-and-toss joint. You had to toss a small wooden hoop, tossing it over an upright block like the end of a two-by-four cut on an angle, short end toward you. If you did, you won the prize on that post. But you had to stay behind a line, If you leaned too far over the counter and landed the hoop on a good prize, it didn't count. Sometimes people argued about that because there were really good prizes. The joint was referred to as the "Knife Rack" because many of the prizes were knives of various kinds. There were pocket knives with varieties of blades and handles including "switch" bladed knives, daggers, hunting knives, "Bowie Knives," and others, all with sparkling, sharp-looking blades, some curved, some straight, with assorted handles of carved wood, celluloid, ivory, rubber-gripped, even a rabbit-foot handle on one. In addition to the knives there were cigarette cases and lighters, cameras, pocket watches and wrist watches, pistols, and even a German Luger, all really good prizes. There was a lot of "flash" to this concession.

People didn't win that stuff very often because the hoop would catch onto one of the blocks when you threw the hoop from the customer's side, and then you lost that chance to win. In order to win, the hoop had to go all way over the block and down to its base. Actually, the only way that hoop went over the block, was when it was placed from back to front. The concessionaire demonstrated what you had to do, but the "marks" didn't notice the tricky way in which it was done. You couldn't possibly toss the hoop over the block from the front. This type of gimmick was known as an alibi game. If someone thought he had won, he was argued out of the big prize with some reason like leaning over too far, or the hoop didn't go all the way down, or some other alibi was given.

The Rexalls had another concession in which bowling balls were suspended from overhead and a bowling pin was placed beneath it fitting into a wooden triangle to make sure it was in the right spot beneath the ball. You had to swing the ball away from you, just missing the pin both coming and going, just as the concessionaire showed you. That was easy, you found, as you took a free chance at it. But somehow your luck changed as soon as you put cash on the line. And even after several more chances, you found that you had lost your touch. The shill who followed you won on his first chance. Do you think that quarter of an inch error in the placement of the pin would have anything to do with your bad luck?

The Rexalls always stayed at the better hotels at fairs. But they had to have their dog with them too. That Pekinese was such a cute little dog but he had the sharpest teeth. He caught me a couple of times as I started to pet him, not badly, just more like a deep scratch. If Mrs. Rexall held him, I could pet him all I wanted to.

There were a lot of other nice people with the show. But first I want to tell you about our opening that year.

The City Lots

WHEN WE OPENED IN GARY THAT YEAR, 1928, AROUND the middle of April, it was still pretty cold at night. We had a couple of days of rain, which didn't help. However, the people around Gary were a stoic group. Many of them were willing to brave the weather. The Gary steel mills were working full blast. The night-time sky and clouds glowed red with the reflection of the blast furnaces melting iron. The soot and dust, the dirt and smoke, the smell and the coughing were all by-products of the mills. Still, the jobs in the mills paid well and were considered to be highly desirable.

Times were good in the spring of that year. These were prosperous times for most people and businesses. People had jobs and had money to spend. One should also note that people were also into saving money at that time. These workers in Gary, working in the steel mills and heavy industries, were mostly white then and mainly of foreign descent. They had known hard times and were aware of the need to save for bad times. But for now they had enough to enjoy some things. Carnivals had always been part of the entertainment in their countries, and so here it was again. And they were hardy enough to endure the chill of April to come out to the lot. They came as family groups. As a result, you were more likely to sell tickets on a ride for a family rather than to one or two riders. Gary wasn't a bad spot, all things considered.

The attendance was good enough that we "cracked the nut" and came out a little more than even. Furthermore, it gave us the chance to complete preparations and organization of the outfit for the coming season.

Millie and I had gone out to the lot with our folks on Sunday. We usually went on Friday or Saturday, and occasionally on Sunday, while we played the lots until fair time. We became reacquainted with the group who were the regulars with the show, including those kids who were around at that time.

Art Pettit was at his usual weekend job in the popcorn wagon so he couldn't hang out with us. Eddytha Dennison was on spring break and was there. Her mother let her go on some of the rides with us. Dempsey and Tunney were not there. They would not start their fights until school was out. They lived in Ohio. I think it was in Sandusky. Johnnie Norman didn't come out that weekend. My cousins all came for that opening weekend. We went on all the rides. Charlotte didn't do but a couple of rides. She was older than the rest of us by a year and so she held herself somewhat aloof from the rest of us kids, but Henry and Esther, and Uncle Louie's kids, Irene and Carrie, went on all the rides with Millie and me. When we tired of he rides, we went to some of the shows.

We all went to see Bob Mercer and Wanda do their riding in the new Motordrome. We stayed for two shows. Their show was really exciting. Then we went to the Penny Arcade.

Mr. and Mrs. Komjathy had started that a few years before. They were Hungarian people we knew and who wanted to do something in their retirement from their wine business in Hungary, so my dad arranged this for them. Mr. Komjathy was a tall, slender, dignified man who stood very proudly and straight and smoked a pipe. He was a kind man but not given to laughing very much. He always seemed to be serious and thoughtful. He had to use a cane because of an old injury to his leg. He patrolled the aisles in the penny arcade to keep kids from messing with things.

Mrs. Komjathy, a very business-like lady, worked as the cashier and had rolls of pennies and nickels for change to give people who wanted to use the machines. She would give us a handful of pennies, and we could use them in their machines. These penny arcade machines were about the size of a slot machine. The idea was to look into the double eye-piece to see a series of slides. They were somewhat like movies but you had to turn a crank. This made the series of pictures flip over fast enough so the people seemed to be moving fast or slowly, depending on the speed with which you turned the crank. They had some good ones: cowboys riding and shooting; Indians chasing settlers in their wagons and shooting at them; hunting bears in the woods, and all that. I didn't care much for the dancing girls and love scenes. The other thing we liked there was the machine which gave you an electric shock. You held the handles and the shock gradually became stronger and you held on until it was too much. I couldn't hold on as long as Henry. There was a punching bag you could hit for a full minute for a nickel. There were scales and we always weighed ourselves. There was a machine to test the strength of your grip. We were not to use the nickel movie machines. They were for older people, and they were about girls in Paris dancing in short skirts, couples hugging and kissing and stuff like that. I know because we looked at them when no one was watching.

We always went to the snake show. We might not stay long but just long enough to see if there were any new snakes. Some snakes didn't live long in the shows and had to be replaced. Also, we wanted to see who was the snake-charmer this year. Sometimes it was a woman but usually it was a man. They would hold the snake and make us pet it. Yuck! I wouldn't want that job.

Emma, the "Fat Lady," didn't have anyone looking at her so we went in to see her. She said she had a good winter and hadn't gained any more weight, just stayed the same. She asked how we were, about school and all that. She was nice.

It was getting cooler and we were hungry so we went to the cookhouse and had a fried green pepper sandwich. About an hour later, the show closed. We all went home. That was the end of our day in Gary. We were in school all week so we didn't get back to Gary. By the next week, the carnival had moved.

Our next spot was in East Chicago. That area was also smoky and dirty like Gary, but now it was from chemical and oil plants, and other factories in the Calumet area. We went there one night, but it was still pretty cold so my mother let us go to a movie with another cousin who lived there.

It was a good movie with Tom Mix and some bad guys who were chasing Tom and his girl friend, shooting at them, so Tom had to jump from his horse, Tony, and get behind some big rocks where he and his girl could shoot back at the bad guys. He got some of them but the rest ran away. Tom and his girl did not get hurt so the next thing you knew they were hugging and kissing and all that stuff. Then he took her home and that was the end. It was good except the hugging-and-kissing part.

There was a good "Our Gang" comedy too. The kids dressed up in old clothes and did a play for the other kids and charged them two cents to see it. One of them had a big black coat and tall hat on, and a long mustache. He was the villain, and he was chasing Farina who was supposed to be a black slave who had run away from his master. The villain and some of the other kids with dogs were helping to catch Farina, but he got away by walking across a river on blocks of ice, but they weren't really ice, just boxes he stepped on.

There was also a Pathe News Reel which showed Herbert Hoover, who was running for president, talking to factory workers to get them to vote for him, and Henry Ford showing his new car, the Model "A."

The carnival moved after a week there. We moved on Sunday night to Whiting, which wasn't very far away. This was very much like East Chicago. Both towns had a lot of oil refineries, highly industrial areas, with well-paying jobs.

These towns were pretty close together which made it easy to move. I heard my dad talking to some of the men about the expense of hiring trucks to move every week. A few years earlier, he had bought some used Packard trucks to do the moving, but they broke down frequently and he couldn't depend on them, so he decided to junk them and since business was good, he decided he would buy four Chevrolet semi-tractors to haul the show.

Until then, we had only a Fordson tractor which was used mostly on moving days and nights. It was used to spot the trailers when we moved, and for loading trains, as well as to haul the trailers and wagons when we moved, but most of the move was done by trucking companies we hired. Now we cold move our own show, making several trips with the semis.

When we moved, late in the day of that last night on the lot, Al Beuse or Dago Louie would start spotting trailers that afternoon close to the point where they would be loaded. Toward the end of the evening, when the crowds had thinned, the help started to do things like removing bulbs, changing clothes, getting their personal belongings together, and then when the word was out to close, they started work in earnest.

Fences, platforms, ticket booths, and all such lighter equipment went down and were placed in stacks to be loaded on top of the heavier things. The tubs on the whip were detached and they were run up channel irons onto a trailer made for that purpose, with a second level area for the tubs. The rest of that trailer was for the iron works and cables to which the tubs had been attached, and finally the engine for the Whip. The heavy steel-plated platforms on which the tubs rode were loaded onto their own trailer. They were heavy and greasy, and it took several men to unbolt each one of them and lift them out over the supporting understructure as they then loaded these onto their trailer.

Finally, the men detached the electrical cables running to the transformer wagon and which by now were carrying juice attached to floodlights by which the men worked. Then they threw the lighter stuff on top with their personal gear, and the ride was ready to be moved. But the help had more to do. They now went over to the baby airplane ride, tore that down, and put it on the trailer too.

This took several hours, and they were tired. There might still be work to be done if anyone else needed a hand. The same general routine went on for all the rides, shows, and concessions. When it was all done, the help threw themselves onto the canvas or other such bedding in the various trailers and slept while they traveled to the next spot.

Early the next morning, the midway had been laid out and after a few hours of rest, they proceeded to put up the ride or do whatever was their primary responsibility. They were ready to open by that night at the new spot. This was the one period of time when they had to really work hard. And they did. The rest of the week they were generally free during the day, doing their personal things and doing the light work of a Carnie that evening and night.

A new show joined us at that time. We had been waiting for it to be part of the outfit, but delivery of certain equipment for it had delayed its opening until now. The new show was to be run by a young Hungarian, a recent arrival in the United States, a friend of Mr. Komjathy's, who had persuaded my dad to give the young man a chance. This young fellow and his wife, Frank and Rosa Dohany, did magic. He did not speak English very well, but she had learned to speak it well in her school in Hungary. Frank was not a big man but he stood very straight and with deeply set dark eyes, a slightly long and thin nose, and a small goatee, he appeared almost satanic. She was a neat looking, small, thin, dark-haired, attractive little lady. When Frank put on his black cape and hat for their act and combed his black hair straight back, he really looked capable of black magic. That and the trace of a foreign accent further enhanced his image.

Frank and his wife put on a good show. To begin with, he tossed coins into the thin air. They disappeared, and he then made them reappear in some strange place like in my ear when he called me up onto the stage. He made cigarettes disappear from his hands and then he'd pluck them out of the air. He showed his hat to me, inside and out, while I was onstage, and when he waved his magic wand over it, a rabbit poked its head out of the hat. He took his red pocket handkerchief out of his pocket and when he waved the wand over it as he held it crumpled in his fist he made it turn blue. He did that once more, and now it was a small American flag. He did other magic too, but the best part was when he put his wife into a small cabinet. She could hardly fit into it. Then he took a half-dozen long swords and thrust them through slots in the cabinet, and after she screamed when he put one sword through, he stopped and pulled out the swords and opened the cabinet and she stepped out smiling. She wasn't really hurt. She had fooled him. When that failed, he tied her down inside a long box, on her back. A man in the audience agreed to come up on stage to help tie her down, and to help saw her right in half and sometimes Al Beuse helped him do that. But they didn't really cut her in half, because when they opened the box, she was still in one piece. Finally, he opened a black closet and made her lie down on a bed, and by waving the wand and saying some magic words which he always had to do to make the wand work, she started to float up into the air. To prove it was not a fake, he passed a hoop around her body both ways and proved there was nothing lifting her up into the air.

I don't know what magic he used, but I learned how hard it is to do magic when I got my magic kit for Christmas that year. I found it didn't have the right stuff to make any-one float in the air like he did. He was with us only that one year, because he got a better job on stage in theatres. As I said, his name was Frank, or as the banner said, "The Great Ference, Prestidigitator and Magician."

We played a number of spots in that Calumet region. These were all industrial towns. There was a wide diversity in the people throughout the area, but they were all regarded as hard and steady workers: Germans, Poles, Swedes, Hungarians, Italians, Slavs, Czechs, Mexicans, African Americans, Filipinos, and others. They generally lived in sections of these cities with other people with common backgrounds. We successively played Hammond, Hegewisch, and Calumet City in Indiana as we wound our way toward

Chicago. Then we hit a few spots around the southeast edge of Chicago and then South Chicago, gradually winding our way, through the city, playing spots like 107th and Ewing, 103rd street in Roseland, 63rd and Ashland, 47th near the Stockyards, and then we moved into the western suburbs including Melrose Park, Cicero, Park Ridge, and others.

After school was out for the summer, we made spots like Wheaton, Western Springs, Downer's Grove, and finally Palatine, as we prepared to head up into Wisconsin for the county fairs.

While we played the city lots, before we hit the fairs, and while school was in session, we kids went to the carnival lot only on weekends. My folks drove back and forth from home to the lot every night. Grandma Bodnar stayed at home with Millie and me when our parents were gone. After school was out for the summer, I went to the lot almost every night. When we made the fair circuit, it was too far to travel the distance daily, so we stayed with our folks in hotels, and occasionally in private homes.

During the times we stayed home, Millie and I did the usual things that kids do, but of course Millie did more girl things. I played ball in the street with the other kids in the neighborhood, or played "knife," (mumblety-peg), with them, rode my bike, made a go-cart, painted my wagon, went hunting for frogs at a nearby pond, watched ants scurrying around their nest, tried to identify birds and the insects we caught using my books on insects and birds, went to the manual training classes and services at the Baptist church, and practiced my violin and piano (as little as I could get by with). On cool or rainy days, I read adventure stories in the *Saturday Evening Post* and *Liberty* magazines, and read Street and Smith's western and science fiction magazines. I also read books like those about Tom Swift, who invented and built a lot of things, and books about Frank Merriwell, who was very athletic and excelled in every sport he played. On rare occasions I might consult the encyclopedia, or sometimes just looked at the sky and the clouds and wondered how and why. Sometimes we dug caves, climbed trees, played war or cowboys and Indians, and in the evening we played Tag or Red Light around the lamp-post on our street. And if we heard the bell ringing at that hour, we rushed home to get a nickel or even pennies to get an ice cream cone, because we knew the ice cream wagon was coming. Daytime, we would jump the ice wagon for a piece of ice to slake our thirst, spitting out the first mouthful because there was usually sawdust on the fragments of ice. I really don't believe any of us used the word "boring" throughout our childhood.

When school was out for the summer, I went out to the lot often. I had a job. I was to run the "Kiddie Airplane Ride." I did that most of the time, but when I tired of that I might sell tickets for one of the other rides unless some of the other kids with the carnival were there. If they were, we did our usual things: the rides, the shows, the cookhouse; and then anything that might be special at that particular spot.

When we played Melrose Park, it was for a church celebration honoring St. Anthony. It was for a Catholic Church, Our Lady of Mount Carmel, in a predominantly Italian parish. We set up on the streets and on the playgrounds. There were a lot of other stands there for food, souvenirs, and the like. We had a second Ferris Wheel join us for that week. The two Ferris Wheels were set up side by side, an impressive sight. The people who owned the second Wheel also owned another ride. This was called the Venetian Swings. There were six boat-like structures, suspended from overhead, each one holding two people who sat in the opposite ends of these boats. The riders sat and grasped the handle bars of a mechanism in front of them. They pulled and pushed on these handle bars, like you do on a Irish Flyer. That caused the boat to swing back and forth. Some people worked hard at it and those boats were flying high, well above the ground. You could make the ride as calm or exciting as you dared. It was fun to get swinging as high as you could.

What I remember most about Melrose Park was the procession on Sunday. That afternoon there was a long procession starting in the church. There were priests and nuns in their ceremonial habits, and other people proudly dressed up in their best, many with colored ribbons across their chests walking in a long parade from the church, through the streets and the midway, and back into the church.

But most important, other men were carrying statues of their saints in the parade. Groups of men were carrying platforms with one or another of their saints on them. People knelt and crossed themselves as the saints came by. These bearers stopped every so often to be relieved by other men who rushed forward for this privilege. When they stopped with the statue of Mary, the Mother of God, people rushed up to her statue. Mary was clothed in a beautiful garment of light blue with gold and silver threads running through it. They showered money on her, pinning bills of all denominations to her clothing and putting money into baskets on the platform on which she was mounted. You could tell that many of the bills were for a large amount of money because the larger denominations of currency had areas of gold coloring on them at that time, since the United States was still on the gold standard for our currency. There were many dollar bills as well as bills for a lot more money pinned to her robe and in the baskets on the platform. There was so much money that some of it fell into the street. No one pocketed the money if it fell. People grabbed the money, put it back in the baskets, knelt, crossed themselves and were obviously pleased with themselves to have done that.

That was our busiest day of the year up to that time. Those Italian people were having the best time. They sang and they danced; there was music everywhere. Everyone was dressed in their Sunday clothes. You could see they had large families and had fun together. People seemed to know each other, and they kissed and they hugged and they laughed, fully enjoying the day. It was nice for us too. Their good time and sense of enjoyment and carefree happiness extended to the midway. They loved those Venetian boats, and they loved everything we had to offer too, especially the rides. We had them lined up to buy tickets, standing on the waiting platforms, the rides fully loaded, all day and well into the evening. We had one of the best days ever.

Toward the end of the day, I could see anxiety creeping into my mother's face. She spoke to my dad about her concerns. He too became rather serious about the matter. As the show closed, the ticket sellers for the rides and the shows and other parts of the outfit began checking in, leaving their money, their ticket bags, and their "take," with my mother. The help collected around the ticket box more so than usual. The word had gone out that we needed them in numbers for protection. When my father showed up in the course of all this, he had good news. He had gone to the police and voiced his concerns, and the outcome was that when we wee ready to leave, the police would escort us to the home of the chief of police. None other than the chief, himself, had offered to have us stay at his home, realizing the danger to us if we followed our usual routine and returned home that night, or even if we drove through the city to drop the money in a night depository at a bank.

A few years earlier, again after a particularly good night at one of our better "spots," my folks had returned home with Al Beuse and Johnny Hence, who also worked for us and lived near us. Millie and I were not there. We spent that summer on a farm near Bangor, Michigan with family friends, the Geresys. Grandma lived with Aunt Marie that summer.

That night, when my folks pulled up to the house, it was late and all was quiet. Johnny headed for home as my folks and Al went into the house. They turned on the lights to see two masked men pointing guns at them. It was a "stick-up." Two men outside had stopped Johnny and ordered him into the house and forced everyone into a clothes closet with orders not to move.

They all stayed locked in there, even after they heard a car pull up and then leave. When all was quiet, they managed to dislodge the dresser, which had been placed against the door, and dislodged the rubber wedge under the door to block their exit. They came out to find the robbers gone, the house ransacked, and the valise with the day's receipts gone. Gone too was my father's big emerald birth-stone ring and my mother's pearls, ruby ring, and other jewelry. It was a frightening and costly experience. Too late they had learned the dangers of bringing the money home late at night as had been their routine up to that time.

Thereafter, they would drop the night's receipts in a depository box at one or another bank at which they had opened accounts. This resulted in an inconvenience which required either that they go to the bank in the morning to do their usual counting and bookkeeping of each of the individual bags of money from the various units of the carnival, or the money would be brought home for accounting, as was the usual routine.

At home, the usual procedure was to count the money in the morning. I can recall that on many mornings in the summer, I arose to find my folks and whoever was staying with us counting money. Each bag was individually opened, the money counted, and the accompanying record showed the amount of the bankroll which had been furnished the operator, his proceeds, and the amount he had withdrawn for personal use. This counted against his salary or percentage, as the case might be. The money was then shoved into a pile while others of us counted the different denominations of coins and bills into stacks of a certain number. Coins were wrapped in paper rolls. The paper bills were sorted into their proper stacks and wound with a wrapper. Millie and I helped doing this too. Meanwhile, my mother did the bookkeeping on this and made up the bankroll for each of the operators for the next night. Then, finally, the money was banked.

My bonus was from the Penny Arcade. There were frequently slugs and strange coins from various countries that kids had probably found at home and used in the machines. I had an interesting collection of these at one time, including buffalo-head nickels, Indian-head pennies, an old Roman coin, and others which I tried to identify by their countries and values. I never found a very valuable coin, although some of them were worth slightly more than their stated value, according to a book on coins which I had. This collection was lost with time and changes of residence.

There was a rather memorable incident that occurred that year. It was at our first fair of the season, in Palatine, Illinois.

The Fairs

THE COOK COUNTY FAIR WAS HELD IN PALATINE. THIS was on the outskirts of Chicago, northwest of the city. We had been winding our way toward Wisconsin, where most of the spots were located on our fair circuit. Palatine was a short move from our last city spot, Park Ridge, so it was easily handled with the new Chevy tractors my dad had bought. The semis could make several trips a day to move the carnival trailers and wagons to the new spot. Once there, Al or "Blackie" would use the Fordson to locate the trailer on that area of the midway where the show or ride was to be erected.

Some of the moves between fairs were over a much greater distance, and then the show was moved by rail. The carnival loaded onto eight and at times up to ten flat cars and a box car. There would also be a coach in which the Carnies traveled. Some parts of the outfit would go overland with a Chevy "semi" hauling a trailer or two. We had more time to move from one fair to the other than we had while playing city lots close to each other and in the same region. Fairs usually did not run an entire week, so we had one or two days each week for travel and setting up. We didn't tear down, move, and set up all in the same day, as we did at city lots.

There were other differences between playing the fairs

and the city lots. Around the city, we operated every night, from about six in the evening to about ten or later at night. On Sunday we played from about one in the afternoon to ten at night. Fairs might run five to six days, usually, but we operated there from about ten in the morning to ten thirty at night.

In the city we were the whole show. At fairs, we provided entertainment, but we were only part of the show. Our contracts with the fair associations included certain requirements about the size of the outfit we were to bring in for our part of the midway, but the fair associations were free to make contracts for other amusements and concessions of many kinds, different from what we offered.

Furthermore, these county fairs were organized not only to bring some fun and recreation into the lives of their people, but they were even more dedicated to exhibiting the agricultural, industrial, and domestic elements of the community in an educational and business-like way.

At times at these various fairs, Henry and I would take in the exhibits. Many of the exhibits were in relation to farming: tractors, cultivators, threshing machines, windmills, electrical power plants for the farm, different feeds for different stock, and in Monroe particularly, there always was a lot related to the dairy industry such as cow stalls, milking equipment, separators, etc. We were on the lookout for booths that were giving out balloons, paper airplanes, pencils, snappers, and other advertising junk

We would tour the various exhibit buildings. If Millie and Eddytha were along, we might go to the home economics hall. Here was the main show of domestic crafts and skills. Sewing and cooking especially. There was competition for growing and making and showing the best fruits, grains, pies, cookies, cakes, dresses, hats, quilts, sausages, and in

Monroe, everything about cheese, especially Swiss Cheese. Here, also, there were booths of agencies dealing with farm needs: insurances, governmental regulatory and assist agencies, conservation information, marketing representatives, and others concerned with the business aspects of farming.

We visited the stock barns of which there were usually several. The cattle were in one, the horses in another. Pigs, poultry, rabbits, goats and sheep, and others were relegated to their respective enclosures. They were beautiful animals. I had my favorites. I particularly admired the Angora rabbits, Black Angus bulls, Clydesdale horses, Suffolk black-faced sheep, the "Silkie" chickens, and big fat Poland-China sows and piglets. The Silkie chickens were beautiful and strange, with their fine silky feathers covering head and face, legs and feet, as well as their bodies, resembling a hairy ball of fur as they sat in their coops.

The air would be filled with the cacophony of the sounds issuing from the various animals, all grunting, baaing, bleating, crowing, snorting, and bellowing, and all was further mixed with their odors and that of sweet smelling hay and the fresh beddings of straw. The horse barns smelled the best to me, the smell of horses and hay, a somewhat sweet and pungent smell, not unlike that of some of the cigars I smoked in later years

It was of special interest to us city kids to see the accomplishments of the farm youth in their 4-H activities. We learned of this great national organization dedicated to promoting the interest and education of these young farm people in the practical aspects of farming, farm life, animal husbandry, and domestic skills. The programs further emphasized other matters pertaining to their lives, including health and citizenship. Here were these young farmers breeding and raising their own live stock, sheep, goats, chickens, calves, and so on. They raised these animals from birth, tending them, feeding them, grooming, cleaning, and showing them. And the girls showed their excellence in their domestic skills, including cooking, sewing, canning, growing their own fruits and vegetables and in other ways demonstrating what a good young woman could do. They earned our respect. Their achievements far exceeded any of our ventures.

Through competition for the coveted blue, gold, and other colored ribbons, the 4-H program sought to honor the young farm people for their effort in raising or producing the best of livestock or for their excellence in home-making.

Business entered the scene, creating a further incentive for the 4H Club winners by purchasing the prize winning livestock, either for breeding or for the market. They also purchased the products of the 4-H members involved in domestic activities such as dressmaking, sewing, baking, gardening, or other homemaking pursuits. This was the bonus for the 4H'ers for all their efforts. In turn it had great advertising value to the purchasers who had thereby demonstrated their community spirit by rewarding the youths for their conscientious work. The kids learned and profited while competing. Further, it was not only youth who was involved. Others also had their prized animals, or quilts, or pies, or jewelry and whatnot entered in these competitions and exhibitions. The fairs rewarded ambition and emphasized the good values in work. This way of life was well recognized and endorsed. These activities were the most important aspect of the fair as far as the community was concerned.

Millie and Eddytha and I went one day to the stock barns at one of the fairs. On that particular day, the sheep and lambs were being judged. In the judging ring were the prized sheep and lambs. They were beautiful animals, so gentle and meek, dressed in soft blankets of wool, bleating plaintively, and led into the ring mostly by young boys and girls. The girls especially seemed concerned for their animals, petting them, combing their wool, and hugging them, knowing that they were not long from being marketed.

One youngster was crying and sobbing as she led her charge into the ring. When the judges awarded her lamb a blue ribbon, she cried even harder, aware that now he would surely be bought by a high bidder and be marketed in the shops.

Eddytha started to get teary-eyed at that thought, and then Millie started too. It all seemed so sad that this prize lamb should be assured of an early fate by that blue ribbon.

Later that day, we learned that the lamb was chosen best lamb of the show, and as fate would have it, a happy ending. He had been bought by a breeder who would raise the lamb for breeding purposes, not for the market. Oh, happy day!

Our girls sought out the girl in the lambs' barn the next day to find her glowing happily with the knowledge that her lamb had been saved for another day. She told of raising it, feeding it, tending it from the day it was born. She had actually seen it being born. She loved her lamb but was now willing to part with it, proud of it, still loving it, but happy to know it was not going to be butchered, and instead, would have a happy life.

Eddytha was very taken by this and showed empathy for the girl and her lamb, which revealed an aspect of her which Millie and I had not had an opportunity to know. We now saw an emotional aspect of her which was not apparent previously. We wondered if this was the result of some deeper emotion which might have resulted from some other experience in her life? Was it because of the divorce of her parents and the periodic separation from one or the other? Could it have been because of her attendance at a boarding school, being away from her mother for long periods? Was she experiencing conflict about her feelings for her father and stepfather?

She had told Millie of how she struggled with the thought of having two fathers. She really loved her real father and enjoyed time with him when she was at school. And then there was Mr. Dennison, who was so very nice to her but toward whom she could not develop the same feeling that she felt for her real father, an emotionally difficult situation for a thirteen-year-old girl.

We saw Eddytha only during the fair season and spring break. She was around all summer so we did lots of things together when her mother permitted and when she did not have to work the fish pond. She didn't really like that work. She knew that she was cheating people with the way she read the numbers on the fish at the concession. She told us how she prayed that this sin would be forgiven when she attended church while at school. I saw her as a really good person, kind, gentle, thoughtful, and sincere. I guess I sort of liked her. She was developing a build too. She wasn't flat anymore.

I remember an occasion when I was on the Ferris Wheel with Millie and Eadie (we called her that sometime). The wheel was being loaded and when the seat at the bottom was being loaded, it was exactly opposite to us and we were at the very top. When we were at the very top, no one could see us there. It wasn't really crowded with three of us in one seat, but to make more room, and since no one could see us, I put my arm in back of the seat where Eddytha sat. She was sitting next to me. She turned and looked at me. I could tell she didn't mind. She wiggled a little as if she were looking around to see things below and then she was closer to me. I took my arm down when the wheel started, but I had a funny feeling when I had my arm back there and when she had looked at me.

For most of that summer I saw her almost every day at the fairs. Sometimes I might go over and speak to her, but most of the time I didn't know what to say to her, so I would just walk by her concession and wave a little to her. She always smiled and waved back. I sort of felt as if she were my girl friend, you know, just like you have boys for friends too, nothing more.

One of the most interesting and scary events of my youth occurred at that fair in Palatine. It was not as impressive as a country fair as those in Wisconsin. This was still close to Chicago, and the fair seemed to be more interested in providing entertainment than its 4-H activities. It did have the usual, big wooden grandstand where they had free acts every night and afternoon. In the afternoon they also had harness races and at night the free acts were followed by fireworks just as they did at all the fairs.

On one night after the regular grandstand show was over, and instead of fireworks, three large crosses in the middle of the racetrack were set afire. The largest one in the center must have been 30 feet high and the ones on each side were just a little smaller. That was pretty scary to see those crosses burning. It was even worse a little later.

I was in our car when this happened because it was getting late and I was sleepy and at those times I would go to our car, lock myself in, and go to sleep. This time the car was parked right behind the whip and next to the race track, so I could see everything and was close enough to the guys on the Whip so I knew I was safe.

When the crosses began to really burn, a long line of men marched out from under the grandstand to the middle of the field. They lined up in a widely curved line in front of the crosses, maybe forty or fifty men, all dressed alike, in white sheet-like robes from their necks to the ground, with a white pointed hat on their heads, with part of the hat coming down to cover their necks and faces, There were two eyeholes in the masks so they could see. During this time, it was all very quiet and really spooky.

I was scared, but I just stayed where I was. I watched and listened.

One of the men, who was their leader, stepped up onto a platform and began to speak into a microphone, so everyone could hear him.

He talked of this great organization called the Ku Klux Klan which he said every patriotic man should belong to if he wanted to keep America free and keep the riff-raff from taking over the country, and how awful it was that the people in Rome were trying to run our country, and of the need to protect our women, and to keep people in their place. He talked for a long time, and finally, they all marched out as the crosses slowly burned down. People left the grandstands rather quietly compared to the usual ending of the evening. Maybe they were scared too. I guess they didn't know what to do.

Nothing more happened about that. My folks told me some things about the Ku Klux Klan. The KKK was preaching hate, they said. The Klansmen apparently were not the good guys they said they were. It was a long time before I heard any more about them. I guess some people believed all that talk their leader gave. They called him their "Imperial Wizard."

The next move was to Monroe, Wisconsin, the Green County Fair. That move was much longer than the jumps around the city, and so the move was by train, except for those trailers hauled by the semis. I watched them load the trains a couple of times when I was allowed to go with my dad.

The railroad cars, flat cars, would have been spotted very close to a crossing in some area away from a lot of street traffic. The trucks would haul the trailers and wagons to the train to be loaded. Only the four-wheeled trailers were loaded onto the train. The semis moved their usual loads overland. Our Fordson tractor was the work horse of this move by rail. The Fordson would hook up the trailer, and get it into position facing two long channel irons on supports running from the street crossing up onto the tail end of the flat cars. Planking was laid between the channels for a man to walk on as he took the tongue of the trailer guiding the trailer up the ramp. The trailer was pulled by a rope attached to the front of the wagon to the tractor on the ground beside the railroad car.

In this way, the Fordson tractor now pulled the trailer up the ramp. Men ran with blocks behind the wagon wheels to prevent the trailer from accidentally rolling backward. One of the men had the tongue of the trailer, guiding it along the channels. These heavy channel irons were a foot wide, had sides a few inches high to help keep the wheels on track. A cross-section of the channel iron would look like a flattened letter "U". It required a dozen or more men to lift one of these channels into place. Once the trailer was on the flat car, it was pushed and pulled along the flat cars to its final spot on the train.

As the wagon was moved forward from one car to

another, other men were between the cars adjusting the alignment of short channel irons to move the wagons from one car to the next while the man at the wagon's tongue guided the wagon forward into place. All of this was repeated with each wagon until everything was loaded and the wheels blocked.

It was heavy work. Dangerous work. Accidents happened. Ropes tangled. Fingers and hands were especially endangered. Wagons missed the channels and fell between cars, and even men did. It was when things went wrong that I saw my father jump into the worst of it, guiding the wagons up the channels and jumping between cars as he guided the wagon from one car to the next. He worked side by side with his men, his example encouraging their flagging energies to keep up with his.

Unloading the train was an easier and reversed order of the same procedure. It was risky work. It was work for real men.

We unloaded at Monroe and set up. Monroe was one of our regular fairs. My dad had the contract to play it for many years. We always stayed at the Eugene Hotel, a small, quiet, dignified hotel across the street from a shop that sold almost any cheese you could want. Monroe was the center of the Wisconsin cheese and dairy industry. Gigantic wheels of cheese were on display along with all kinds of lesser amounts of the great assortment of cheeses made locally. My mother routinely went there our first day to stock up on various kinds of cheese and bread to savor during our stay there. That was a real treat.

Henry and I looked forward to this spot. We had learned from the locals of a swimming hole on the nearby Sugar River. Al Beuse or some one of our men would drive there with us for an afternoon of fun. The river had a firm, slightly gravely bank and bottom, not a mushy bottom. The water was brown in color as most rivers are, and a little on the warm side in midsummer. A rusty, old bridge carried the road across the river here, maybe about twenty feet above the water. The local kids swimming there were bold enough, some of them, to jump from the bridge into the river, which wasn't really very wide nor deep, at least not of a depth to dive into safely. We swam and we played but never mustered the daring to make the jump. With luck, Henry and I might get there twice during our stay in Monroe. He was the only one of our cousins to make the fairs during the summer.

There was a pony ring at this fair. The fellow who ran it owned some eight ponies of various sizes and kinds. For a dime, kids could ride the ponies around a ring for five minutes or so, but no running them nor whipping nor kicking them, so it was a pretty tame ride. If kids were too small to handle the pony, someone led them around the ring a few times. Henry and I hung around until we landed the job of doing that for a few hours. That gave us the privilege of riding the ponies back to the barn at night, and we were allowed to run them a little going back. Then we went back to get the next ponies so we could also ride them back to the barn. Henry and I raced, but these ponies weren't really fast and didn't want to run very far. But they were the real thing. You couldn't beat that.

We spent at least one afternoon in the grandstand at each of the fairs. There were usually about five free acts: a dance team or chorus line, acrobats, trick bicycle riders, some unusual musicians such as the one who played the musical saw, and always a clown or comedy team for laughs. I still remember one song that I heard at several of the fairs that year.

"The whale swallowed Jonah, throwed him on the land,
but if the fool swallowed me, he might not understand,
so I'm a gonna stay, right where I oughta be,
cuz I ain't a gonna let no whale, make no sandwich outa me."

That was show biz at its rural best for that day.

Harness races were run before the show and between acts. Sleek but fine-muscled trotters and pacers pulled the lightweight, bicycle-wheeled rigs with a usually splendidly attired wizened driver, hands held high gripping the reins, urging his charger to do its ultimate best with a fixed gait. There weren't any bookies or betting windows, but there probably were some in the crowd who felt they could spot good horseflesh and were willing to bet their neighbor on that. These people loved their animals and appreciated the racing for just what it was meant to be: a test of breeding, training, speed, and skill.

The evening show was followed by fireworks. The skies were colorfully lighted with showers of blue, green, red, silver, and gold embers shot into the night sky, then wafted down to earth with the breeze, the ooh's and aah's punctuated by the aerial bombs which shattered the night. There were times when the night was brightly lighted by one or more magnesium white flares released from the bombs, carried along by a parachute floating lazily across the heavens. On the ground we could count on great "Roman Candles" with their Vesuvius-like fountains spewing floral arrangements into the sky, fiery outlines of cows and chickens, always Niagara Falls, and finally closure of the program with the brightly blazing American Flag accompanied by the band's thrilling version of the Star Spangled Banner. Everyone stood and then left the stands, happy to be an American and in such a good and plentiful land.

When the stands let out, there was usually a brief spurt of business on the midway, and then it was over for the night. Some of these people had been there all day, a big day at the fair, a once-a-year outing. Only the exhibitors did more. They came early and stayed the length of every day looking after their animals or their exhibits but also enjoying the fair.

The next jump was to Madison, another of our regular spots for many years. It was done with our own trucks and transportation, since the distance was not great. We usually stayed at the Fess Hotel there. It was on a side street and, as on so many streets in town, you could go to the corner and look straight up the street to see the State Capitol, pretty close in appearance to our Capitol in Washington, D.C.

We toured the Capitol with my mother one day. We were part of the typical group that tours such places. Our guide was very good at giving us the history of the development of the state, explaining the great frescoes, the sculptures, and other art in the various chambers, relating their significance, and relation to historic events, most with the usual bands of Indians pictured in the background of the main figures in the paintings.

Madison was and is a pretty city with its Capitol, and other government buildings, its four lakes, and its great university situated on Lake Mendota close to the center of the city. This was a prosperous area, in agriculturally rich farmlands of the Midwest, and adjacent to the plentiful tourist- and sports-dominated lakes dotting the state northward of it. Henry and I had hoped to swim in those lakes, but the state health departments at that time warned that the threat of polio seemed to be greatest in bodies of waters such as these. So, we did not have that pleasure there despite the plentiful bodies of water.

Business was always good there, so the price of admission on the new ride, the Lindy Loop, which commanded great interest in its first year at that fair, was raised to twenty-five cents. Although "good times" abounded in those years, the farming communities were not participating in the generally great prosperity flooding the rest of the land. We did well there, but my folks spoke of the noticeable lesser degree of spending on pleasure in the rural areas compared to that in the cities. And, as we later learned, the farther north we went, the farther from the larger cities, the more rural and agricultural the area, the less prosperous became the regions and their fairs.

At these larger fairs, our midway consisted of the active carnival but there were also many other attractions. There were always a lot of food concessions. Salt-water taffy being pulled and kneaded by big-armed machines right in front of your eyes made you want to get a bag of those for sure. Candied apples and snow cones, cotton candy, five-colored rainbow ice cream cones, hot dogs and hamburgers, wiener schnitzel and brats, orange drinks and soda pop, all fulfilled their promise of better living and eating for that day.

But if you really wanted to eat, the best deals were the meals served by the various church groups. The fair at Madison had six or seven of these church sponsored dining tents. These were an all-volunteer, fund-raising activity for the churches. It was all home-cooking with many of the dishes brought in by the ladies who had cooked up the pies and other dishes at home.

Each church would have a large tent with tables, chairs, and counters, and all the equipment to do some of the cooking. Food was served at long tables with family-style servings, which might include any combination of fried chicken, roast beef or pork, mashed potatoes, green beans, corn on the cob, sausage, meatloaf, barbecued meats, cheese and pasta dishes, tomatoes, cole slaw, potato salad, carrots and peas, and other local produce, with each church vying to give you their best. Then there was milk, coffee, lemonade, iced or warm tea to wash that down to prepare you for watermelon, several kinds of pies, cakes, strudel, and cookies, home-packed peaches, pears, and plums, "and maybe you vant some whipped cream or ice cream on top. Ja?" Yes? "Dots goot." That Svensky woman certainly made sure you were satisfied. Not too bad when the whole meal cost only about thirty-five cents. Our own cookhouse couldn't match that.

In addition to the food concessions and our own concessions, the fair board arranged space for a variety of other stands, such as photographers and fortune tellers, and those selling souvenirs, balloons, lottery tickets, airplane and balloon rides, camel rides and miscellaneous others, sometimes even other shows and rides. Bruegel himself could not have added to this scene of a county fair, and this was pretty typical to a greater or lesser degree of all the fairs on our circuit.

Our next stop was Portage, Wisconsin, a short hop from Madison, and in the region of "The Dells," Wisconsin's picturesque area of sculptured geological formations, hills, and ravines, with their exposed strata of Cambrian sandstone, colorful and interesting.

It was a little out of the way, but my dad took us touring

in our Huppmobile to see "The Dells" on our way to Portage. The "Hupp" was a pretty dependable, heavy, car. It had a vertically oriented rear trunk, and we had added a detachable expandable fencing on the left running board to carry more luggage. Inside it had a ceiling light and on the side partitions there were small vases to hold flowers which they never did. It was all pretty modern.

There were some interesting sights on that trip, undulating layers of multicolored sandstone and rock which had been exposed along the sides of the cliffs and ravines by the rush of water in prehistoric times. This was a great tourist attraction for the area. As a result, the roads were crowded and there were a lot of business places scattered along the way, marring the natural setting of the area. It was still a nice opportunity to see the beauty of that part of the country.

We finished the trip and went directly to the fairgrounds. My dad went right to work, laying out the midway, designating the sites for each part of our outfit for our part of the midway. The semis were pulling in as we arrived, and some had already parked their wagons and trailers and gone back to Madison for more. The Dennisons and the Normans and some others sat around on crates and boxes, and bags of canvas which had already been unloaded. They were comparing notes on the trip and the interesting geological formations and strata they had seen. Someone asked: "How did all this come about?" Johnny Norman's brother, Charlie, who had been sitting there reading, turned and read to us from a brochure about "The Dells."

"At one time, several hundreds of thousands of years ago, as the last ice age ended in that period of Pleistocene glaciation," he told us, "all of this was covered with water forming an immense lake referred to as Lake Algonquin."

We couldn't understand how that had created "The Dells."

He read further: "The glaciers covering the area had melted and formed this large lake. As the water retreated, parts of the underwater mountains were exposed and ground down. This sediment was then re-deposited as varied and interesting layers of rock and sandstone. As the water ran off, it formed channels for rivers and some was left behind as small lakes, and some of the residual was large enough to form the Great Lakes. All this took thousands and thousands of years. As the water retreated and flowed into other areas, some channels of water cut into the sandy ground and made the ravines, rivers, and streams we now see, also exposing the various layers of the earth and hillsides."

That was interesting to all of us, and we were glad to have it explained, but I had trouble imaging anything taking so many years.

We listened intently. Then I asked, "Where were the dinosaurs and the Indians while this was going on?"

"Oh," he said, "this was long before the Indians, even before there were men on the earth." I tried, but I had difficulty imagining the world of that time.

The ladies were jabbering away, as they usually did. Mrs. Norman was worried about her dog Ching. "He's been so out of sorts, lately," she complained. "These road trips just don't agree with him."

"Even dogs must feel the stress of the irregular living we go through," said Mrs. Dennison. Everyone agreed on that.

About that time, Mrs. Rexall came along with her feisty Pekinese. The minute he saw Mrs. Norman's Chow, he started to bark and strain at his leash, trying to get to the much larger dog. The hair on Ching's back bristled a bit. He was obviously annoyed by this mindless chatter of the barking Pekinese. "He just wants to be friends," said Mrs. Rexall.

"Just so he has no other ideas," commented Mrs. Norman. Everyone laughed. I didn't want to see them fight either. "I guess we can let them get a little closer." Both ladies relaxed the leashes a bit. Tiki ran up to Ching, smelled him all over, and gave a sharp little bark.

Ching had stood motionless while Tiki was going through this ritual. He stood stiffly, legs rigid, staring straight ahead. When he heard this last little bark, he relaxed, lowered his head and the dogs touched noses. Ching took a couple of smells of Tiki too. I guess he liked what he smelled because then everything was okay between them. Tiki barked. Ching had gotten the message. Tiki said he wanted a friend. There weren't many opportunities to have a kindred friend when you're on a leash, traveling around the countryside all the time. Ching barked back, "Let's play." The two of them immediately started straining at their leashes circling each other, the little guy jumping at the big guy, then threatening as if to spring at him, the other lunging forward as if to eat Tiki alive, but both animals with their tails wagging wildly with the pleasure of their new-found company.

We kids had listened long enough to this lady talk, but we liked watching the dogs. We asked if we could take them for a walk. Wish granted, we took them by their leashes, and walked around the grounds. My dad and Al and some of the ride and show owners were going along the staked-out line of the future midway. My dad was measuring off spaces and assigning them to the various entities of the Show.

"Where will your fishpond be?" we asked of Eddytha.

"We won't know until my dad comes back. He's over

there with your dad, trying to get a good spot near the Merry-Go-Round. Kids hang around there a lot and many of our customers are kids, so that's a good spot for the fishpond."

A stray dog showed up just ahead of us. He was a black dog, skinny, almost as big as Ching. He came toward us slowly, with his head low, ears flat against his head, tail hanging low and motionless. That didn't look good to me. We shortened our leashes and dragged our dogs over to the side away from the other dog. The two larger dogs began to growl, a real low grrrring sound. The Pekinese ran under the chow, between his legs, and then he started to growl too. I didn't like the way this was going.

"Let's get these dogs out of here," I said. I was afraid they would get into a fight. "Beat it, get out of here." I shouted at the black dog. – "Take off. Git!" He stopped, stared at me, then backed away a distance and took off. Ching was still growling, his hair on end, and straining to get after the other dog. We decided we'd had enough of that and went back. The ladies were still jabbering away. Boring, even if we were never bored otherwise.

This fair was new to our circuit. It was in the center of the tourist and recreational region, a land of many lakes, many with good fishing, and areas for good hunting when that was permitted. The Dells was the center of these sites of geological wonders we had just learned of, but industrially and agriculturally it was poor country.

After a couple of hours, things were organized enough that my dad took us to our hotel in town. Eadie and her parents were staying at the same hotel where we had arranged to stay, so we saw each other a lot at breakfast and other times that week. However, the big deal for Henry and me was the knowledge that there was a good spot for swimming in the Wisconsin River close-by.

The fair didn't open until the day after, so the next day Henry and I walked out to the edge of town, picked up some bread and milk and sandwich fixings. We went to the spot we had been told of on the river. It was a really nice place to swim. You could see the sandy bottom through the clear water and the beach was of nice, soft sand The river was fairly wide but you could almost wade across it to a sand bar island which had some scraggly bushes and trees growing on it. We fooled around in the water for a while, swimming and jumping around. We were the only ones there.

It was about noon by now so we made our sandwiches and had them with a milk chaser. We knew we had to rest for a while before we went back into the water so we were just sitting around after lunch when we heard a loud "Hi there." We looked around and there was Al Beuse with two young women. I wasn't surprised to see Al because he was to pick us up later in the afternoon, but I didn't expect him to bring ladies to the place. I didn't know them but I did recognize that they were from the girl show which had joined us for the fairs. I remembered seeing these two with two others when they were on the bally. They did the "shimmy" up there for the tip. I had also seen them in the show once. They were younger than the other two ladies in the show and they also had more "built." They put on some acts in the show, dancing and singing and doing some acts with a guy dressed up funny like a clown. He made the audience laugh when he told stories about them and pretended to pat the girls here and there in their act. They didn't let him get away with it, and he always jerked his hand back as if he had burned it when he touched them. They put on a good show but the inside talker always promised the final show on closing night would be a much more exciting one. Everyone was invited to attend for a slightly higher price of the

Left: My father with his new Ferris Wheel.

Below: My father standing, John DeJung in booth.

Above: My father and
mother on the top; Mr. and
Mrs. Norman on the
bottom.

Right: My father on the left,
Louie Berger in the middle,
and Mr. Dennison on the
right.

Right: Maggie and Jiggs Abroad, a fun sideshow ride.

Below: Bob Mercer and the Wall of Death

Page at left: Top: Engine trouble; left to right: Al Beuse, "Dago" Louis, and unidentified, the "Dumbie," and Little Johnny.

Center: Mr. Komjathy in front, "Swede" selling tickets, and Johnny Hence on the left.

Bottom: "Farmer" and the Lindy Loop.

This page: Top left: Uncle Henry and his Chair-O-Plane.

Top right: Eddytha (right) and a schoolmate (left).

Right: : Henry (left) and me.

Top left: "Whitey" on left, "Blackie" top center, Mr. Carson on the right, and me at age 6.

Left: The "Farmer" on the left, me at 12 years old, and Little Johnny on the right.

Above: Here I am astride one of the ponies at the Ring.

Top left: The "Dumbie" operating the Whip.

Above: Riders leaving the Whip.

Left: Millie (in front) and Esther in the Kiddie Airplane Ride.

Left: Uncle Louie (waving his hand) operating the Ferris Wheel.

Below: Uncle Mike selling tickets on the Ferris Wheel.

ticket. I never saw the "blow-off," as that final show was called, but I heard it was almost the same as the usual show.

"Meet my new girl friends," said Al. He introduced us to them. Their names were Isabelle and Rose. We stood up and shook hands and asked if they wanted a sandwich.

The girls said, "Oh yes. We are hungry. We haven't had lunch. We're famished." And so the sandwiches didn't go very far as they ate what little had been left after our first lunch.

Isabelle asked us how old we were. She seemed surprised to know we weren't even teen-agers. "I'm 23 and Rose is 27," she said.

"We've taken dancing lessons since we were your age." said Rose. "We took ballet too until we started to put on weight. It runs in our family," she said. They were cousins, just like Henry and I, and had taken dancing lessons in the same place in Chicago. "Our school turns out very good dancers," she proudly announced. "Many of the dancers had very good contracts, some even with the Muriel Abbott Dancers at the Palmer House. This job with the carnival was just for the summer to make some money for school in the fall." Of course it was well below their dignity to take such a job, but it was only temporary until they finished some more lessons. They also had to take off some weight to get the better jobs. "Those other two girls with the show think they're so hot. One of them says she played the Rialto. I don't believe her. She's not that good. Besides she's too skinny for the outfits they wear in those shows." Rose obviously had a case against those other "girls" in the show.

In time, the girls asked about the water. "It's fine" we said, "nice and warm. The water is pretty clear and there's a nice sand bottom, not mushy like a lot of rivers."

Isabelle turned to Rose and asked, "Shall we go in?"

"Of course," said Rose, "That's what we came for." And with that they removed their outer clothing and revealed that they had their bathing suits on underneath.

Al did the same and we all ran into the water. The girls whooped and hollered when they first hit the water because it wasn't as warm as they expected. It wasn't very deep so we just swam to the middle, a short distance, and swam back to shore. Mostly we were just playing around in the water, splashing each other. Pretty soon, Al swam under water and grabbed Rose by the legs. You should have heard her scream. She really thought some fish had her. She scolded Al and then laughed.

"Don't scare me like that," She said. "I know there are fish in these rivers, and I don't trust them. Isabelle and I swim in Lake Michigan at home. There are fish in there too, but they never come near you. It's a safe place to swim. I'll bet there are lots of things in this water, probably turtles and crabs and all kinds of stuff. I wouldn't want to have one of them grab me." We laughed at that.

Henry and I thought that would be fun too, so we started swimming under water. The girls would really scream if we came up near them, especially if we touched their legs or if we came up under them and knocked them into the water. Isabelle was really having fun with us, but Al and Rose became tired of it and swam to the island to explore it.

Henry and I sat on the beach with Isabelle. "Where do you live?" we asked.

"In Chicago," she said.

"We live in Chicago too. Where do you live in Chicago?"

Isabelle said they were "in the Rogers Park District." That was a pretty nice part of the city, near the lake, up on the North Side. We were South Siders. They asked about our White Sox and then bragged that "the Cubs represent the North Side and are in first place!"

I told them, "I hope they can keep it up. The Cubs are well known to crack up in the second half of the baseball season."

By the time Al and Rose returned, it was time to go. Isabelle gave Rose some mean looks because Rose had gone off and left her, I guess. We all got into our car and Al took us back to the fairgrounds.

Portage had a nice fairgrounds, but it was not a generally busy fair. This was not the best agricultural area as far as land and crops and with the poor prices farmers were getting for their crops, it was no wonder that we did not find it a particularly busy or profitable fair. As kids, that didn't bother us. If we weren't busy we did other things. If there was work, we did that.

Our jobs were not really demanding. Usually, our duties were such that we could walk away from them and have someone else take over. Henry helped his dad by selling tickets for their Chair-O-Plane part of the time. Johnny Norman tended the stock wagon for their concessions and could lock it and walk around while keeping an eye out for shills who were returning prizes they had won. Millie helped in the snow-cone stand. I've already told you of Eddytha, Art Pettit, and others and their jobs. I was to be in charge of the Kiddie Airplane Ride, but I tired of it after a few weeks, and wrangled a job helping "Dutch" Rogers at his Bingo game.

"Dutch," was really a nice guy. He was older but not real old. He was divorced and lived with a lady in the Englewood area of Chicago. She never came to the carnival. I didn't know her at all. Dutch was always relaxed, always the same, not a driver. He was a nice guy to work for but he had a funny scar on his left upper lip. When he talked he had a strange voice as if he were talking through his nose. My folks said he had a hare-lip when he was born and that it was repaired when he was young but some defect persisted inside his mouth causing his voice to come out that way.

Bingo was played in this rather large joint, about twenty by forty feet, under a tent, with fixed stools on which the players sat. It was open on all four sides. It was usually set up in the middle of the midway in such a way that people had to walk around it on one side or the other so that maybe they would decide to sit down and play.

The winner of each game could pick one of the dozens of brightly colored Indian patterned blankets hung from the rafters of the joint. These were "Genuine Beacon Indian Blankets." That was our spiel, as we called out, "Hey! Come in. Play Bingo. A winner every time. Win Genuine Beacon Indian Blankets." Well, they were pretty good cotton blankets but not made by Indians. There are no Beacon Indians. They were made by the Beacon Indian Blanket Manufacturing Company. But they were "Genuine."

"Dago" Nick worked for Dutch too. When it was busy, all three of us would work. Otherwise, Dutch or I would take off. Cards were ten cents, three for a quarter. Kernels of corn were used to mark the squares as the numbers were called. When we had enough players, Nick would shake the jar of numbers and pull one out, call it out, and mark it on his master card. We would repeat the number so people at our end of the joint could hear it: "Under the B, eleven; under the G, fifty two," and so on. When someone called "Bingo," we hollered, "Hold your card; there could be a mistake." We checked the winner against the master card, and if it was okay we announced, "Hey! A winner! The lady [or gentleman] wins a Genuine Beacon Indian Blanket. Take your choice." Then we'd pick up the cards and prepare for the next game.

They were great guys to work with, always cheerful and ready to laugh. But Nick did have problems. He was one good-looking Italian. I heard him speak slowly and softly to some of these good-looking girls who might stop by and he would forget he was selling cards. He forgot about Bingo and Dutch would tell Nick to "get rid of them." Nick would tell them to come back at quitting time, and sometimes they did. This was not a problem to Nick.

Toward the end of the day, when business slowed, old Grandma Norman, that nice, gray-haired, dignified, motherly appearing lady came along to play. She usually won the last game or two. Then she would take her blankets and turn them in to the stock wagon. Nick had peeked at her card and "threw a cop."

We went next to Menominee. This was the last fair of the year for us kids. It was near Labor Day and school started the day after. The fair at Menominee was also just okay. It was not as extensive as the fairs in the larger city areas. However, there was a greater sense of neighborliness at these smaller fairs. People seemed to know each other better. They greeted each other like old friends, sat around talking and laughing and sometimes seriously discussing other matters. This had been timber and lumbering country, but the best stands of trees had already been cut so that work wasn't going too well anymore, and the land was not the best for agriculture, so the area was not particularly prosperous. And yet folks looked forward to the fair each year and were ready to spend a bit to enjoy the seasonal occasion.

Menominee had a lake near the edge of town where Henry and I rented a boat and spent the day. The small lake was almost fully devoted to duckweed, but we did find a few clear spots where we could swim off the boat, which we did. But mostly, it was a matter of rowing around the weedy lake, enjoying nature, watching the fish dart through their beds and the water beetles as they skimmed the surface of the water, catching sight of deer in the distance, and sensing the clean air.

At the boathouse we city boys saw our first chipmunk. He had suddenly darted out of the brush, stopped a second, quickly appraised us, and was gone. He looked like a small squirrel, but those yellow stripes along the sides of his head and body gave him away. I'd seen pictures of him in books, but this was a real live chipmunk. Now that's not much of an animal to be thrilled over, but when you've never seen one in nature and you turn around and find one scampering ahead of you as you leave the dock, you sense that you have seen something special. I guess you have to be a nature lover to feel that.

Otherwise, we just did our usual things. The week passed. It was time to go home. We said our goodbyes. We had a last fling with Eddytha. We rode the Whip, with Eadie between Millie and myself. We were thrown together a lot on the curves. The Tilt-A-Whirl was even better. There was some gentle up and down to this ride, but mostly you were thrown around in a small circle sometimes one way and then the opposite way. Either Eadie was thrown into me or I was thrown into her. We didn't mind. We took our last ride on the Lindy Loop. That was almost tame compared to the others. The ride whipped you around a circular, sharply hilly track in the seating console on rocker arms. This meant up and down, while rocking back and forth on the rocker arms as the centrifugal force threw Eddytha against me. She felt warm and soft to me whenever we were thrown together. She and Millie shrieked as girls are expected to do in a situation like that. That was our last bit of fun on the road for that year.

The next day Henry, Millie, and I were put on the train for Chicago. We each had a name tag with some information on it, some luggage, some sandwiches, and a promise from the conductor to my mother that he would see that we were well taken care of. We had the two seats facing each other at the front of the coach. We also had a cardboard box with some lettuce leaves and carrots in it with a white rabbit Henry had acquired.

As the train pulled away, my mother cried and Millie cried a little, but not for long. Pretty soon we thought we should see how the rabbit was doing. We peeked in the box, and Fluffy, (that was the rabbit's name) poked his head into the opening, sniffed, looked around and then pulled back into the box. He had not eaten anything so we tore up the lettuce for him. We thought he might be thirsty so we put a paper cup of water in the box for him. We watched him take a sip and then he sat up and just looked at us for a minute. He was moving his nose around a lot and his ears too. Millie thought he was trying to tell us something.

It was warm on the train so we opened the window. The air felt good but smoke and dust blew in so Millie closed the window. Henry wanted it open so he opened the window again. Then he reached into the box and took Fluffy and held him. That made Fluffy nervous and he was shaking a little so Millie tried to hold him. Henry closed the window because he did not want the rabbit to get loose and jump out the window. That was a good thing because suddenly the rabbit jumped out of Millie's arms onto the floor. Before we could get him, he was hopping along the aisle, sniffing here and there, and by the time we caught him. he had laid some little marbles under the seats. Henry grabbed him and sat down quickly because the conductor came through the door and saw the rabbit.

"Where did he come from?" he asked. "From that box," we said. He looked at us rather strangely and told us we were not to have an animal in the coach. It was against the rules and he could lose his job if he didn't follow the rules. "But," he said, "if you keep him in the box and no one says anything, we will pretend he is not here." That sounded good to us so we put him in the box and let Fluffy start eating. We could still put our hand under the cover of the box and pet him.

We took turns doing that for a while. Then when people started falling asleep, one of us would watch for the conductor while one of us took the rabbit out of the box and held him. He only got away once and didn't jump out the window or anything; he just roamed around the floor, sniffing around until we picked him up again. I saw the conductor coming from the other car, so we put Fluffy back into his box. The conductor wanted to know if we were getting hungry. He said there was a car up ahead that served food and that it was about time to eat. So we said, "No, thanks" and then got out our sandwiches and ate them.

Soon a black man in a white coat came along and wanted to sell us something, so we all bought some chocolate milk and a candy bar with the money we had for the trip. He asked if our rabbit had food and water. At first we asked, "What rabbit?" After he laughed we said, "Yes." He left and we took Fluffy out again.

A lady with a big hat came and asked if she could she see our rabbit. She said she loved rabbits and drew pictures of them on cards for the company she worked for. We let her hold him and pet him a little.

After a while, we were getting sleepy, so we took turns sleeping and watching Fluffy. We were hungry again when we woke up so when the butcher (that was the name of the black man in the white coat) came again, we all bought a Coca Cola and a sandwich. The conductor said we would be in Chicago before long, to get ready to get off at the end of the line at Union Station.

When we arrived there, Grandma Bodnar and our neighbor, Matt Uhlian, met us. Matt took us home in his car. Aunt Susie and Aunt Marie and all their girls were waiting for us. Everyone said they were glad to see us and asked, "How was the trip?" We had to kiss them and after we said "Hello," we told them about the rabbit. They were surprised and then they all had to hold Fluffy and pet him.

We left Henry and the rabbit and went home with Grandma. She was to look after us until our folks finished the fair circuit. They had only a few more fairs to play. The next day I was back to playing ball in the street with the neighborhood kids. I told them of my summer and they told me of theirs.

The most important thing was that they had dug a cave in the empty lot across the street, with a tunnel and trap door entrance. They would let me in, but first I had to donate some candles because it was too dark in the cave to do anything and since this was a secret society, we would need light to have our meetings. I found some half-used candles at home and was then given full membership in the secret society. I was back in the old routine. The fair circuit was over for me for the year. School started a few days later.

Between Seasons

SCHOOL STARTED THE DAY AFTER LABOR DAY. CHICAGO schools were different then. One could start school at five years of age either in the fall or with the start of the spring term. I had started in the fall but skipped a half year in the fifth grade, and so I was now in the second semester of eighth grade. My teacher for this semester was Mrs. Fisher. She remembered my dad, whom she taught in the fourth grade. He had to quit school after that to help work on his father's farm. That's when he learned things such as the slaughtering of animals, which became his winter occupation for many years. I think I liked school because I made good grades and that made people think I was smart. I had to do it though to keep up with Charlotte and Henry, who were in the same class. Irene was there too.

It didn't take long to get back into the school-day routines. We were out each day at three o'clock, went home for a snack, then out to play, and homework at night. My grandmother was there to look after us. She was getting old and gray. She moved slowly but was still able to do the housework and cook for us. We spoke Hungarian with her and ate her good Hungarian cooking. There's nothing better than chicken paprikash and maybe nut or prune jam kifli pastries. She was pretty liberal with us, but then again, I don't think we gave her much trouble.

We played baseball on the street in front of my house after school. When a car came along the road, everyone shouted, "Car coming." We stood to the side as it passed, then we went back to play.

A few weeks later we began playing football. There was a small park, a grassy area, about a block away at the Pennsylvania Railroad Station. We would go there to play tackle football. Otherwise, we played games of passing or kicking in the street.

The Chicago Bears had a really good team then. So did the University of Chicago. They were called the Monsters of the Midway. We didn't have a good radio at that time to listen to the football games. I did have a crystal set which Uncle Mike gave me when he got his radio. I could only get one station, KYW, and it was too scratchy to listen to, but Uncle Mike had a good one, a Crossley Superheterodyne, and we could listen to the football games on his radio. It would be another two years before we had our own radio.

I remember the first football game I heard when we got our Atwater Kent Radio. It was the Notre Dame-Southern California game. I was pulling for Notre Dame. The names of certain players in that game are still fixed in my mind. They were Frank Carideo, Marchmont Schwartz, Joe Savoldi, and Marty Brill. Notre Dame won, 27 to 3. They were called "The Ramblers" at that time. They were National Champions in both 1929 and 1930. They had made a great comeback after the 1928 season when they had only 5 wins and 4 losses. Their coach was Knute Rockne. That was the year he told the team of the Gipper's last request, and they went out and beat Army "for the Gipper."

On Sunday we would go to West Pullman Park to watch

the park teams play. Our team had a real good player. He was red-headed and refused to wear a helmet. He sure was tough, but he did get knocked out a lot.

A few weeks later, the carnival had completed its Wisconsin circuit and was now at Crown Point, Indiana, playing the Lake County Fair. This was a really big and important fair. The fairgrounds had solid brick buildings for showing stock and for 4-H activities, as well as for commercial exhibits such as cars, tractors, farm equipment, and the like. There were usually a lot of other concessions selling food, souvenirs, balloons, and whatnot.

This was the fair where there had been the exhibits I mentioned earlier about venereal diseases and Siamese twins.

There was always a gypsy fortune teller at that fair. An old gypsy woman would have a small tent with a glass globe in it. This old gypsy sat in front waiting for someone who wanted to have their fortune told. There was usually a young girl too, dressed in a gypsy outfit like the old woman's. She seemed to be looking for men who wanted their fortune told. The man with them was a short, dark-skinned, mean-looking old man with a big moustache. He hung around but not right with them all the time. I stayed away from them. I had heard how they kidnap children. The people like those from Gary and others of European background were mostly the kind of people who had their fortunes told.

The grandstand acts were good here: a line of dancing girls, trapeze artists, a clown band, that fellow who played music on a saw, and two men who made jokes about each other. There was also the usual harness racing and fireworks, but they also had a contest for horses pulling heavy loads to see who had the strongest team of horses.

There was something else very special about this fair. It was the only fair we made that had automobile racing. This was held only on the last day of the fair. These racing cars went zooming around the dirt track, kicking up dust, their engines roaring, cars sliding around the turns, sideswiping each other, their motors exuding the smell of the special motor oil which was said to be castor oil for those high-powered motors, tires blowing, cars smoking, threatening to catch fire, other cars falling out of the race with mechanical problems, with the survivors being proclaimed the winners. There weren't any bad accidents, but in all, it was an exciting event.

Millie and I were there only from Friday afternoon to Saturday night. After the last day, we went back home with my mother and dad. Usually, Crown Point would be the last fair. The show would make one more spot, and after that it would go into winter quarters.

This year was to be different. Louie Berger had persuaded my dad that the circuit should be extended, taking at least part of the show south, to warmer parts of the country. The show could be cut down to our four main rides and could be hauled overland, making good use of our new semis. Louie, the Jew, had lined up a six-week tour of various celebrations and fairs, ending in Biloxi, Mississippi. And so the season was extended. My dad took the show south. My mother stayed home with us. Uncle Mike had lost his job in the factory, so he went along to do the work my mother usually did, looking after the money and the books and selling tickets on the rides.

Well, the outfit finished the six-week tour and returned. This year it went into winter quarters in an old, abandoned sugar-beet factory in Riverdale. There was plenty of room for all our equipment indoors for the winter work. One area was walled off by canvas and kept warm with a big pot-bellied stove on which a coffee pot was always available. In those days people used a lot of sugar and cream or milk in their coffee. Canned milk was used, and I still associate the taste of canned milk with that place. A lot of painting and repairing was done there over the winter.

There was one bad accident with all that work. One of the men was using the electric circular saw we had bought when we built the Motordrome. He used it carefully, but all in a second, he made a careless move and the saw ran into his knee. He was rushed to the hospital and had surgery and eventually it turned out pretty well since he had only partially cut into the kneecap and the actual function of the knee was not affected. That was a close one. I wasn't there when that happened, but I thought a lot about how tragic that could have been.

Henry and I did a lot of exploring in the old warehouses. They were three and four stories high and almost a block long on each side. The buildings were used mainly for storage of boxes for a candy company. There was an engine room with one of the biggest machines I had ever seen. It was a steam engine with one wheel which was about twenty feet in diameter and a governor almost three feet wide. It hadn't been run in years. It was just fun climbing around it and trying the various levers that didn't work. The factory was located on the Calumet River. We played around there a lot, trying to build a raft. It is probably fortunate that we never built one that we thought was safe enough to turn loose for a ride on the river.

A lot of other things happened about that time. For one thing, I heard my folks talking about the trip south. Apparently that had not turned out well. People in the South did not have it as well as the folks up north, especially the Negroes. Those people who did come to the carnival did not seem to have much in the way of extra money to spend at a carnival. Louie the Jew's experiment with the extended season was costly to my father. Even the slaughter-house business was not as good that year. In fact, a lot of people were concerned about business conditions, worrying about their jobs.

There were other bad things going on in the world at that time. Congress had passed an amendment to the Constitution prohibiting the sale of alcoholic liquors. Prohibition had created a void which would be met by gangsters who brought alcoholic liquors into the country in various ways to satisfy the demand of those seeking such drink and the pursuits that went with it. Then the gangsters made war among themselves to control this criminal activity. The stakes were high enough that they resorted to killing each other if necessary and many were killed.

The worst occurred on February 14, 1929, in Chicago when seven gangsters of "Bugs" Moran's North Side mob were massacred by Al Capone's South Side gang. "Bugsie's" men were lined up against a wall, and executed with machine guns in a North Side garage.

For a long time the mobsters managed to stay one step ahead of government agents who were trying to stop the gangsters and enforce Prohibition. This didn't really end until Prohibition was repealed several years later.

We weren't affected by all this. We were not involved. Our lives went on as usual. For us kids, that meant school. I graduated from West Pullman public school in February of 1929 and entered Fenger High School. It was a large public school with good scholastic and athletic records. I was not an athlete. I was in the ROTC and played violin in the school orchestra. I had a pretty good voice, so I had some leading roles in several of the musical productions of the Glee Club.

There were a lot of other things going on that interested
me at that time. Babe Ruth was one of the heroes of the day.
He hit 60 home runs in 1927; he hit only 48 in 1928. The
Yankees won the World Series just as they did the last two
years. This was Ty Cobb's last year. He retired with a lifetime batting average of .367. "Red" Grange, the great football player at the University of Illinois, who ran for five
touchdowns and passed for another in a game against
Michigan in 1924, was now a star player with the Bears.
Bobby Jones won the four tournaments for the "Grand
Slam" of championships in golf. Jack Dempsey, our great
heavyweight champion, lost to Gene Tunney for the second
time this year but everyone felt it shouldn't count because
Dempsey knocked Tunney out and the referee didn't start
counting Tunney out at first, and this action became known
as the "long count." Tunney then came back to win the de-
cision. A man in Italy named Mussolini had taken over the
rule of the country. In Germany a man named Hitler and a
group of his followers were stirring up trouble over the conditions of the people and the government after they had lost
World War I. Herbert Hoover had been elected the thirty-
first President of the United States.

We went through the winter with my dad slaughtering
hogs and supervising the work in Riverdale in his spare
time. When spring came, the show was ready again to hit
the road.

1929, The Year We Opened in Harvey

WE OPENED IN HARVEY IN 1929. IT WASN'T FAR FROM OUR winter quarters in Riverdale. It was a very nice community, more of a white-collar community like the suburbs north of Chicago, not a heavy industrial area where a lot of workers had been laid off. Harvey still enjoyed relative prosperity that spring. We set up on the streets and an adjoining park near the center of town. The town was celebrating some event in its history and they needed the carnival to add to the entertainment for the event.

It was a good spot to start the season. It was close enough to the winter quarters to make the move an easy one and convenient for running back to Riverdale for equipment or other reasons. It seemed that the first spot always required additional coordination to get the outfit functioning for the season. It was also close to home, probably only about seven miles. Also it was always an advantage to have solid level grounds to set up on. The rides especially had to be leveled before they were put up and that was easier done under those conditions. Further, one could always expect some rainy days in the spring, and again this was in April, and the rains would not cause a muddy lot since we were on the street and in a grassy park.

We looked forward to the reunions at the start of the

season and the opportunity to greet the returning help and other carnies.

Charlotte, Irene, Henry, and I hiked to the lot from home on Saturday as part of a program at school to get us interested in such activities. We had knapsacks full of food. We stopped four or five times to eat a little as we walked. It was a pretty fair distance to hike, about seven or eight miles. We were tired when we arrived at the lot in Harvey, but we had a ride back with our folks when the day was done, so it wasn't really too bad.

The only thing new that spring was a "fun house." My father had bought this new attraction to satisfy certain requirements of the fair associations which always wanted some new shows and rides. It was named "Fun on the Farm." It was entirely contained in one trailer which unfolded and when set up, it presented a two-story front with the appearance of a bright yellow barn, with the heads of horse and cows appearing to look out of the windows and stalls. There was an opening to what would be a hay loft centered at the upstairs level.

One entered through a doorway stepping onto a moving floor, alternate planks going to and fro as one walked over this treacherous floor only to walk next over a series of jiggling turntables in the floor. These revolved back and forth, and then led through a short tunnel which was a revolving drum on its side. Then one passed in reverse direction down a dimly lit hallway accompanied by groans and screams along the way as lights suddenly popped up to illuminate ghastly skeletons and fierce looking animals. A circular stairway now led upstairs where one entered and groped through a maze of pitch black hallways which soon opened into the area of the loft door opening. As one passed by this area, there was a sudden blast of air from beneath. This pleased the crowd of voyeurs attracted by the screams of the young ladies as they ran through the area, holding down their skirts. Next came a ride down a circular slide to come out on a platform which suddenly tilted downward after a few steps and then out the barn door back to the midway, the ladies and girls laughing and screaming and the men stoic and undeterred.

It took Henry and me a number of trips through the "fun house" before we could do the entire route in a few minutes.

This was a good opening spot and the weather was fairly good at this time, so the show had a reasonable play for that early period of the year.

The next spot, Chicago Heights, was said to be a center for activities of the Capone gang. We had no problems, but there was a feeling in the air that the people who came out there were of a different cut. They enjoyed the rides and the shows, and they especially liked the gambling concessions. They were a somewhat rough crowd. This was just outside the Chicago city area, with some farming and industry, but not really part of the Calumet Industrial area.

The Dennisons were there with their "Big Six" wheel. Their man operating this, Mr. Carsons, had a good play every night. This was a beautifully constructed wheel about five feet in diameter with figures of dice, two in each slot all the way around the wheel. The payoffs came when the wheel stopped at the marker with the combination of dice, which you had selected from the layout on the counter. It was somewhat like shooting dice with different odds for various combinations. It was a percentage wheel, not a "flat" wheel, with odds stacked against the players, but with everyone feeling they had a chance for better odds.

Eddytha had her spring vacation the next week, so she came to be with her mother. She was in this all-girls academy and had to wear a school uniform every day. It was a Catholic school, and she was a Catholic, but a different kind, she said. Her own church which she attended with her father, was called the Greek Orthodox Church. She said the Mass was very similar to that of the Roman Catholics, but there were differences in the beliefs of the two churches, such as having married priests, which were not allowed in the Roman Church.

My mother had been a Catholic, but when she married my father, a Protestant, she was not allowed to consider herself Catholic. Those were the rules of the Church at that time. She went to church anyway. Millie and I went with her sometimes, and sometimes I went with the kids in my neighborhood, but I also went to the Baptist and the Lutheran and the First Christian Church at times: the Baptist because they sang a lot in their services, and they also had a manual training program in the summer; the Lutheran because I knew a girl who went there, whom I sort of liked; and First Christian because they had an orchestra in which I played the violin. They also had great Bible classes and stories on Sunday.

Millie and Eddytha and I went through the fun house a couple of times. I liked to go ahead and then jump up and scare Eddytha in the dark hallways. I'd jump up and grab her, and she would scream and laugh. That was fun. Sometimes I would hold her and make her fight her way loose.

After Chicago Heights we went to more or less the same spots we played the previous year. Calumet City was one of them. It was another wide-open town, and the gambling went well there too. The other towns in the Calumet area were the ones we usually played, like Hammond, Gary, East Chicago, Whiting, and South Chicago. However, they did not give us the usual play this year. The factories in that area were heavily involved in the steel industry, and there had been some layoffs in the area, so people did not have the extra money to spend with us.

We had a problem one night in South Chicago, and that may have been because people were tighter with their money and felt worse if they lost it gambling. That one night, some fellow who had been gambling at Kiki Tyler's joint, which had a gaff wheel, became upset when he just couldn't seem to win, and Kiki's wife who "shilled" for him won several times. The mark figured out that he was being taken for a ride and demanded his money back. Kiki wouldn't do that. It was against the code. Mr. Norman came over and tried to persuade the "mark" that the gamble had been undertaken without forcing him to do so, and if his luck was bad that night, it was understandable that he would feel badly, but the money had been gambled and it was lost.

The fellow left, still disgruntled only to return the next night with a half dozen of his steelworker buddies, fresh from the local speakeasy. They approached the stand as a group and again gave Kiki the ultimatum to refund the money or else. They meant business and were not about to stand around idle about this; that much was obvious.

My dad saw what was developing. A quiet buzz went around the grounds rather subtly and hurriedly. There was no calling out of "Hey Rube" as you see in the movies. No one had picked up iron or wooden stakes with which to persuade the offended, but I knew Al Beuse had a pair of brass knuckles because he had let me try them on once. My dad had a lead-weighted flexible blackjack for emergencies. I had played with that too. When you hit it over your thigh, it wrapped partially around your leg and gave it a good jolt.

I'm not sure they had those things with them when this all started. In minutes, the rides had stopped and were unloaded. The help walked off, and in no time there were fifteen to twenty carnies surrounding Kiki's joint. Johnny Norman was there cajoling the town group, advising them against any rash action. A little pushing and shoving developed, but the townies saw they were outnumbered, and before any punches were thrown, the police arrived in response to a call my dad had initiated.

A police sergeant dispersed the group, threatening to throw everyone into jail for disturbing the peace. It was over. Calm was restored, but the sense of trouble remained. Business virtually stopped for the night. We were glad the calm lasted through the next night, after which we moved on to the next spot.

My father always felt money paid to the right people in advance of such situations was money well spent. A little afterward too is quite helpful.

Then we started toward Chicago and the western suburbs. One of the things I remembered about the trips to the lots out there (because we did the same thing the year before) was that on the way to the lot, we would stop at a roadhouse. It was in Wheaton or Downer's Grove or somewhere in that region. I can remember the nice, quiet-looking, two-story house with a lot of cars around it, and going in with my dad and the other men with us. There inside was a large room with a long dark-brown shiny wooden bar with a brass rail for your feet. There were a couple of spittoons on the floor, and a few tables and chairs in the corner. Everyone just stood at the bar and drank.

You could really smell the beer, but I found it didn't taste very good when my dad let me eat the foam from the top of the beer. I didn't like that bitter taste when we made home brew either. I got over that in later years. The men had only one beer and you could tell they felt as if they had really defied the law. They said the "fix" was in, that there was no worry about Prohibition there. Instead of beer, I would rather have a "rainbow cone," which was popular then, with six or eight slabs of different colored ice creams on a big cone.

It was understood that Al Capone, the notorious gangster, supplied the beer and liquor to these places. He wasn't nearly as famous to me as Babe Ruth or "Shipwreck" Kelly, or a lot of other famous people I had heard of. I saw "The Babe" when my dad took me to a see the White Sox play the Yankees. Everyone called him that, but I didn't see a home run that day.

One of the people famous at that time was "Shipwreck Kelly," the famous flagpole sitter. He sat on a flagpole for 23 days and established a new record. He was the best there was at flagpole sitting. Flagpole sitting became a fad. All around town, people and kids were setting up platforms on poles and in trees, in imitation of this record setting fad.

We didn't have a flagpole in our neighborhood, but there was a tree we kids often climbed in a vacant lot on our block. We thought that tree would be a good one for sitting. There was a good fork in the tree, pretty high up, so some of the kids in our block and I established our platform there for tree sitting.

It was only big enough for three of us. Some of the kids were afraid to go up that high, but three of us, Marty, Jimmy, and I, decided we would sit there. Some of the other kids would have to bring us food. Some bodily functions could be taken care of easily. We hadn't figured out all the details on that. We planned to tie ourselves to the tree at night so we wouldn't fall out.

And so we started our sitting one morning. It was a nice, warm, sunny day, only a light breeze was swaying the tree, nothing too scary. We talked about how we would probably have our pictures in the paper when we set a record for tree sitting. We felt hungry pretty soon, so Millie brought us some cookies from home and we pulled them up with a rope and a basket. We had to get rid of Millie when we had to pee into a bottle which we lowered on the rope. Trouble was that none of the other kids wanted to help us with this. They didn't want to touch the bottle full of pee, so there it hung. The platform was pretty hard so Millie brought us pillows from home. We pulled those up. We talked up there, but there wasn't much else to do. Mostly we talked to people who walked by, explaining that we were out to set a record for tree sitting. There weren't too many people to talk to. After a while one of the kids brought us a deck of cards. We played some easy games, you know, like war and rummy.

By now it was noon and time for lunch. Jimmy decided he didn't want to set a record with us and so he went home for lunch. Millie brought sandwiches for Marty and me. Then Marty had to go to the "John." He couldn't do it up there so he went home. That spoiled it because if you came down, you were out of it, unless you wanted to start all over again and you couldn't count the first time toward your record. Those were the rules. I was alone up there. Millie and the other kids had gone home to eat too.

Then, the worst part of it was that my mother came home from shopping and found me up there. Well, you know how that goes. She made me come down, and so we never did get to set any records for tree sitting. That was okay. We decided to play ball instead that afternoon.

We didn't play Melrose Park that year. That church wanted a different carnival every year, but there was another big Italian community right in Chicago that we had lined up for St. Anthony's Festival at Sangamon and Taylor. We set up in the streets near the church, right in the city. It was a big festival all right. They did the same things we had seen in Melrose Park, the procession from the church and through the streets, with the statues of Mary and the Saints and putting money on them, but here we had a different experience.

This area we learned was an area of tough gangsters, several gangs of them, who were very close to each other. A group might come along and if the guy's girl wanted to go on a ride, he was glad to take her on, but he wouldn't buy a ticket. He and the girl just walked by the ticket taker who was pushed aside, and if he tried to do anything, he knew that he might get roughed up by the guy or some of his buddies who had been strolling with him. They came up and decided they all wanted a free ride too, and so stand back or else! Our people didn't do any pushing or shoving. They were smart too. Better to give a few free rides than get messed up.

By the third night, calm returned. My father located the leader of the strongest gang, the "42 Gang," and paid them off to keep peace. Thereafter, everyone in the neighborhood showed their respect for the gang. They knew who was in charge and there was no more of that trouble.

But one night, one of the Carnies, who had been sleeping in one of the concessions, awoke to the smell of gasoline. He lifted the tent flap and looked out to see someone going along the row of concessions sprinkling them with gasoline. Our Carnie shouted the alarm and chased the would-be arsonist, who fled before he put a match to the tents. The guys stayed up to see that he didn't return and to be certain that fire did not break out. An arsonist? A poor loser at the games of chance? Who knows? That was a close one.

I guess that should not be so surprising in that neighborhood. Two nights later, the guys awoke at their usual time in the morning and came out of their tents to find a black man had been stabbed, killed, and dumped in the street. The police showed due, but not unusual, concern and concluded he had been killed elsewhere and dumped there because there was no pooling of blood about the poor fellow. Once again that year, we were glad to move to the next spot.

After paying off the "42 Gang" this was not the grand financial bonanza that the Feast of St. Anthony had promised to be.

We usually played Cicero every year, and we did this year too. The people here were essentially respectable, hardworking folk. A lot of them were Bohemian, and most were employed in the immense Western Electric factory nearby. They made telephones and a lot of other electrical equipment in common use. We had no trouble there, in spite of the fact that Capone's headquarters were right there in the Hawthorne Hotel on 22nd Street. Everyone knew that, and he and his men came and went freely, and he wasn't even Bohemian. But he "owned" the town, and no one bothered him.

However, even in Cicero, there had been layoffs at the factory, and people weren't spending as they usually did. This proved to be much the same pattern at all the spots as the season went on. Apparently business and prosperity were sliding downhill everywhere. The farmers seemed to be the worst off, and President Hoover, who replaced President Coolidge that March, didn't help them. He said they should stand on their own two feet. I remember a quart of milk was ten cents and a loaf of bread was the same. Those big, jumbo ice cream cones were fifteen cents. The carnival rides and movies were still only a dime.

I didn't get an allowance. If I wanted something like an ice cream cone, I had to ask and get a nickel from my parents.

I usually got it unless it was near time to eat. My folks weren't stingy, but they weren't loose with money either. And about that time, I started to notice their even greater concern about money. I overheard them talking among themselves of the money they had borrowed to buy the trucks and the Fun House, and they were still paying on the loan used to buy the Lindy Loop. They spoke as if the times were getting worse, and they were worried about keeping up their payments. However, they felt the fairs would help because they generally were more profitable.

The suburban spots we played on the way toward the fairs were still pretty good. The people in these areas were not factory workers in the heavy industries and their jobs were apparently still holding up well. They were still fairly loose with their spending, and so things were looking better. And we still had the fairs to look forward to. My folks spoke hopefully about the coming fair season.

Season's End

WHEN IT CAME TIME TO HIT THE SUBURBS, NORTH AND west of the city to bring us closer to the location of our fairs, it became apparent that we were in Cubs country. The Chicago Cubs Baseball Team was having a winning season and as the baseball season went on, the Cubs won the National League Pennant. I was glad for them because they had some really good players, but we were "South Siders," and so our loyalties were really with the White Sox, who weren't doing so well. Anyway, we had to keep our fingers crossed for the Cubs because it would not have been unusual for them to "blow" the lead. They did lose the World Series to Philadelphia.

We hit the fairs about the usual time, in late July. The fair circuit was somewhat different from last year. We started this time in Beloit, Wisconsin, since it was about halfway between Wheaton, our last stop in the suburbs, and Monroe which would be our following fair.

What I seem to remember most about Beloit were the mayflies. Beloit is a river town, and this was the time of year for mayflies to emerge from their larval stage and live in the real world for twenty-four hours. The air in the downtown area was full of the dainty critters intent on their sprightly duties of mating and propagating as they enjoyed their brief lifetimes. You didn't dare open your mouth while walking the streets or you had a mouthful of them. And they were not very tasty either.

The day after we arrived there, the shows and concessions were all up. The rides were going up. Johnny Norman and I had nothing to do, so we went to the area to which the empty trailers had been moved, alongside each other, in a row along the edge of the fairgrounds. We went over to engage in one of our favorite pastimes. We climbed up on the wagons, jumping from one to another, daring each other to do more and more dangerous things, until we tired. We decided to rest on top of one of the higher trailers.

As we sat there, Johnny talked about his brother. "Charlie has decided to go back to school in the fall." His brother was tired of just being a shill for the concessionaires. "He said he wanted to be something."

"Like what?" I asked.

"Oh, he doesn't know. He just wants to do something else. He likes going to school. He had good grades in high school."

"Is he really smart?"

"Sure he's smart. He had a chance to go to the University of Chicago. He was near the top of his class at Hyde Park. It's one of the best high schools in the city."

"I never thought he was very smart."

"Oh but he is." said John. "He's always got his nose in a book when he's not on the lot. He'll read anything he can get his hands on."

I remembered he had read to us about "The Dells."

I had never talked much with Charlie. He was older and didn't seem to have much to do with the rest of us kids. In fact, he wasn't really a kid either. He had been out of high school for a couple of years. "What's the use of going to school if you don't know what you want to be?" I asked.

"He doesn't care about that. He just wants to be smart and learn about everything. He wants to be like those smart professors who know so much and just sit around talking about stuff and teaching it. He says they are philosophers. Some of them are psychologists. He wants to be someone like that."

"That's OK, but what do they do to make a living? Is that their job? Do they get paid for just talking all the time?"

"Charlie says they do other things, mostly like looking up things in old books, to learn what was said and done in olden times. He says that is research, finding out about stuff that the smart people had said and written in the past." Johnny seemed to understand all this about his brother. I didn't. "I'm going to go to college," I said. "But I know what I want to learn. I'm going to learn how to make medicines and run a drug store. I'll mix stuff together to make things to help sick people. You can sell the medicine and make money for doing your job. Besides, helping people is a good thing to do, especially if they're sick and you help them get well. That's what I want to do. I'd really like to be a doctor, but that's too hard."

"Not me," said Johnny. "I had a chemistry set, but you couldn't make much with it. That wasn't fun. What I want to do is to build things like buildings and bridges and all that. I do it with my Erector Set. I build all kinds of things with that when we're home."

"Henry wants to do something like that too," I added. "That's why he's taking mechanical drawing next year. He may be an architect or an engineer."

"Art Pettit's good at radio and electricity. He made his own radio with parts he bought from a catalogue. I listened to it at his house last winter. It's not very good, but better than the crystal set Uncle Mike gave me when he bought his Crossley. Now that's really a good radio. Five tubes! You can really hear things on that. You ought to hear Amos and Andy, and Jack Benny, and the Jack Dempsey fights. You can hear the President's talks on it. They have a lot of music on it too, Guy Lombardo and Rudy Vallee, operas and all that. They even broadcast football games like Notre Dame and Army. Art says we will hear a lot more about radio, and he wants to learn how to make better ones."

We'd been sitting up on top of one of the trailers, the double-decked one for the Whip, and decided to move around, so we jumped from it to the next trailer, and then a couple more and then down to the ground.

We walked over to the cookhouse. It was still early. Not yet time for dinner. The show wouldn't open for a few more hours. We ate a hamburger sandwich. It must have been on the grill a long time because it was hard and dry and greasy, very dark brown, but we ate it anyway. It wasn't too bad with a cream soda.

Beloit was a small fair and was the first spot for two new shows which had joined us for this part of the season. One was an animal show.

Circuses have a lot of animals and animal acts. Carnivals do not. Carnivals provide entertainment with rides, side shows, and concessions. However, one of these new shows with us was a "Dog and Pony Show." It had played vaudeville acts in the past but was now a carnival show. Under its top there was only one small ring and two bleachers for seating. The owner, trainer, and ringmaster of the show had three ponies, a monkey, and numerous dogs of different breeds doing a variety of acts.

The ponies were trained to do drills and formations in

response to the crack of a whip. They also did acts in the ring, sometimes with the monkey or a dog on their backs, as they pranced through their routines.

Sometimes the monkey rode on a dog's back or the monkey would ride a bicycle around the ring, tossing kisses to the audience. At one time the monkey clambered up the center-pole, refusing to come down until the ringmaster produced a banana, which the monkey peeled and ate. He was cute in that little red suit and hat he wore.

The dogs sat on little pedestals until it was time for their act, except for a small white poodle which jumped off his pedestal repeatedly, trying to get into the acts with the other dogs, barking wildly whenever he was chased back to his pedestal. The dogs rolled over; they played dead; they jumped over one another; they danced in little skirts; they went over high jumps and through hoops, all directed by a slight motion from their trainer.

The final act was a dangerous one, and the ringmaster indicated what a courageous animal it took to do it. There was a hoop about two feet off the ground which was set afire. The dog for this act was to jump through the flaming hoop. The dog ran to jump through the hoop but he stopped at the last second and wouldn't do it. The ringmaster held him and petted him until the dog felt ready to try it again. But the dog wasn't really ready. He tried half-heartedly and balked again. Then the ringmaster asked the dog if he would do it just for us. The dog barked and nodded his head that he would. The ringmaster said that everyone had to clap to encourage the dog to do it for us, so we clapped, and the dog ran around the ring, and then to the end of the tent. Now he turned around and ran at full speed toward the blazing hoop. He gave one big jump and was through the fiery hoop safely. We all cheered and clapped. The dog ran around the ring barking excitedly until the trainer caught him and put him back on the pedestal.

Finally, the trainer said the dogs wanted to thank us for coming and immediately they all started barking and wagging their tails until the trainer pointed his whip toward the tent flap and they all ran off to their kennels.

The show was over. We wanted to pet the dogs, but the trainer explained that this was not allowed. The dogs had to be kept under strict discipline, not varying their routines, to help them keep their minds on their work. What kind of a life is that for a dog?

Millie and I had gone there with Eadie. We went back with her to work the fishpond with her mother. We hung around there, fishing for a while, and pretty soon some other kids and people came by to see us fish. Eddytha and her mother were helping us fish. Not surprisingly, Mrs. Dennison found that one of the fishes we caught had a big number, so we won one of the big prizes, a cuckoo clock that really worked. Eddytha showed us how to wind it with the pendulum so that a little bird came out of its house every hour, cuckooed and then went back in. The people watching all this decided they wanted a cuckoo clock too, so they began to fish, but they weren't as lucky as we were. Eddytha gave us a new clock, still in its box, as we went off, walking around the midway with it until we could return it to the stock wagon.

We knew what had happened when we won the clock. Eddytha's mother had "thrown a cop" to us in order to interest other people in playing. It wasn't honest and we knew it. I remembered how Eadie felt about it too. It hadn't concerned me in the past when I learned of such things being done as part of the workings of the concessions, but this time was different because we had actually participated in the mockery ourselves.

I recalled too that the Bingo game with which I had worked last year had an element of cheating and dishonesty with it. I thought about this many times after that. I learned to hate the thought of being part of it. A simple game of chance didn't seem too bad, even when you knew the odds were against you. That was a known risk, but to be fleeced by trickery was not honest. I wished that this business could be conducted otherwise.

I knew my folks were hard working people and in time I came to realize they had little education and no talents with which to make a living otherwise. Others might be better able to do well under proper conditions, but my folks were survivors, in a sense, and their hopes for a better life for us, even their wish for me to have an education, which would liberate me from the type of work in which they found themselves, led them to rationalize this as their destiny, their life's work. Fate was to change this in time, but it did bother my conscience.

There was another show which had joined us for the fairs. It fit this same category of activity which was disillusioning me. It was a "Geek Show," the "Wild Man from Borneo." "Mongo" had been "captured in the wilds, a totally primitive man, uncivilized, brought to the states to learn our ways, to adapt to our customs, and become civilized and educated. He was being shown to the public for their edification until the process of the study of him by anthropologists and psychologists, and the process of civilizing him was to begin at a famous university later in the year." That was the spiel of the grinder.

The show consisted of the wild man being shown in a

wooden, paneled enclosure about thirty feet on a side and twelve feet high. There was a viewing platform surrounding the four sides of the enclosure, enabling one to look down into the pit where the wild man was kept. In one corner there was a small hovel with a straw floor where he could rest and even have some privacy at times. He had a crude three-legged stool to sit on. There was also a stump of a log for sitting on or maybe to be used as a table. In the pit with him were a few chickens and a cat. There was also a box with glass sides in which a snake lay coiled on straw bedding. In one corner at our upper level was a platform extending over the pit on which his keeper, in pith helmet, open-collared khaki shirt, bush jacket, and shorts, armed with a bull whip, kept watch.

The wild man himself was a well-built, muscular, but stocky man with Negroid skin and features. He had a big head of curly black hair, grown profusely into a straggly and bush-like mass. He wore an animal skin, probably from a leopard, extending down from one shoulder into a short skirt-like arrangement, which fortunately also had a pants and jock-strap animal skin attached to preserve his modesty. He had an animal skin belt around his waist with a crude-looking axe suspended from the belt.

We went in to see him a number of times. Once when no one else was there, we found him sleeping in his hut. When he awakened, he quietly went over and picked up the cat and tenderly petted him; his keeper just sat there staring out onto the midway. As more people came or when there was already a crowd, Mongo appeared to become agitated. He paced the floor; he tried to climb the walls; he made loud, fierce growling sounds; he chased the chickens with his hunting axe drawn; he grabbed the snake and made threatening motions as if to throw the snake at the crowd. At times he would take his stool and a log and put these beside the wall and attempt to climb up the wall, trying to escape. His keeper had to really work on him then, snapping the bullwhip overhead with a loud crack, shouting at Mongo, throwing things like fruit at him, which Mongo just ate or threw back at his keeper. Anyway, he didn't care, and yet at other times he might get real mad and try to throw his chair at the keeper. Or Mongo would shout loudly and fiercely or scream. He might shout some gibberish, which was probably in the Borneo language, so no one understood it. The keeper finally would get Mongo calmed down. At such times he might cower and creep into his hut. At other times he would growl and scowl angrily at the crowd and the keeper. It was pretty scary at times.

One of the worst times occurred when he caught a chicken. This only seemed to happen about once a night when there was a good crowd present. He spent about ten minutes chasing the chickens with his axe in hand. He finally caught one. He put his axe away. He petted the squawking chicken until it became quiet. Then he hypnotized it waving his finger slowly back and forth in front of the chicken's eyes. Then he laid the chicken on the stump. He stealthily reached for his axe. Everyone screamed as he quickly raised the axe and came down square on the chicken's neck. The head fell off. Blood spurted. He grabbed the chicken and showered blood on his chest. He fell to his knees and bowed up and down to the dead chicken as if this were a ritual practiced by his tribe in Borneo. He became very calm after that.

The keeper threw down some wet cloths, and with a lot of gruff commands and snapping of the bullwhip, he made Mongo clean up his mess. Mongo quieted down after that. He went to stroke his cat or he might just quietly hold his snake, or he would just sit there scratching here and there, picking at his hair, crushing whatever he found between his fingernails.

Some of the crowd would leave now while he seemed to be resting. As new people came in, he gradually became more active, and he started doing some of those same crazy things he had done before. But he only killed one chicken a night.

I had a strange and interesting experience involving him at a later date. I had gone to the fair early with my dad and then had taken ill. My dad had matters to attend to, so he had one of the men take me back to the hotel in our car. I didn't know this fellow. He was dark skinned and he wore a turban, so I guessed he was from India. We talked on the way back and I found out he was from Milwaukee, and he had gone to college for two years on a scholarship in the school of drama. He lost that when he was falsely accused of attempting to rape one of the coeds.

He didn't really like his job with the carnival, but it was the only work he had been able to find, which was in any way close to acting and the field of dramatics in which he was interested.

That's when I found out that "Mongo" was driving me home. I was scared when I discovered that, but only for a second, since I knew now that Mongo was already civilized, and not even from Borneo.

That was an enlightening experience. In time I recognized it to be another of those aspects of our life, the trickery, the fraud, the dishonesty, that filled me with revulsion. I was not comfortable when I thought of these things. Perhaps I should have simply accepted it as show business, an act, a fiction, for entertainment. Nevertheless, I resolved to do my best to avoid such actions in my life, actions which might in any way be considered unethical or dishonest.

In keeping with that resolution, a rather fortunate change occurred that summer. I wanted to work the Bingo game with "Dutch" and Nick, but I didn't want to be part of the dishonest aspects of the game. Well, "Dutch" had seen a new approach to the game that made the it more interesting and also made it honest. It also involved participation by the player so that he too was aware that the game was honest.

The customer threw a ball into a bin which was divided into seventy-five little cubicles the size of the ball, and all the squares were numbered to correspond to the Bingo numbers on the game cards. The bin was on wheels on a track and we moved it along inside the joint giving each person a chance to throw a ball into the bin. With each throw, we called out the number of the little box in which the ball had landed, just as we had done when picking out numbers the old way. This was continued until someone won.

Everyone could see the slot in which the ball had lodged and check the winner with us. It was a new idea, and it worked. People liked playing Bingo with a sense that they had some degree of control over the numbers called. They tried hard to throw the ball into the slot for their number, but they rarely succeeded.

Again, the winner was awarded the choice of our "Genuine Beacon Indian Blankets." They were colorful and attractive to our devoted Bingo players. There were no shills this time for the final games. If there were not enough players to profit us, the game was cancelled, although there were a few times when we did play a final game for a slight loss.

We made Monroe and Madison again. We had our usual fill of cheese in Monroe. The Swiss cheese was so good. I liked it best between two slices of pumpernickel, when it had a good strong flavor. I can still taste it.

In Madison we stayed at a "bed and breakfast," rather than going the distance into town to stay at the Fess. This was closer to the fairgrounds, more convenient, and I think less expensive. My folks seemed to be more concerned about money than they had been in the past. It seems that we just weren't getting the play we expected. Expenses continued, but people were just not as free with their money as they had been. There was talk of people losing their jobs and of others going out of business. There were still good crowds of people at the fairs. The shows in the grandstand were free with the admission to the fair, and they were filled, but the rides and shows weren't that busy, and Madison was the best of our Wisconsin fairs.

After that, we played the Fond du Lac County Fair. This was a pretty big jump, so it was by rail again. Our semis and trailers took some of the show overland. They made the move in time for everything to be up to open on schedule. This was not one of our regular stops, but as a fair, it was quite good financially. It was not as much an agricultural community as some of our other fairs, but it was a progressive business community with a diversified economy and also one of the vital recreational areas of the state. This made it a more prosperous area and we needed that. It was a pretty good jump to our next county fair at Shawano, but we managed that with our semis and with the rental of a few trucks. That made it less expensive than moving by rail.

There was a lake not far from town in Shawano, and we had a chance to swim there. The beach was small but sandy and the water dropped off gradually, making it safe for the play and amount of swimming that we did. The Dennisons had rented a place on this lake for the week that we were there. They had a rowboat with their place so we spent a lot of time in the boat.

I remember once when Eddytha and I rowed away from the beach without Millie. Little sisters are okay but there are times when you wished they would leave you alone. We managed to do that this time. There was a bath house some distance out in the lake where the water was deep and clear for good swimming.

We headed for that. I rowed the two of us out there in the lake, and as I was rowing, Eddytha decided she wanted to row too. She came over and sat next to me, and we both rowed. The boat wasn't very wide so she had to sit close to me. Her thigh was against mine. Her skin was nice and smooth and warm. After a while we were just rowing around in the lake, not trying to go anywhere. Then we took a rest and just floated around.

I leaned back to change position and put my arm across the seat behind her. She leaned back too and as she did, she turned toward me with her face close to mine. If I had been that kind of a guy, I'll bet I could have kissed her. But I wasn't taking any chances. What if she got mad? What if someone saw us, although we were quite far from shore now? Anyway, I thought I had better get back to rowing. So she did too.

We rowed out to the bath house. It was small, set up on stilts, with only two small dressing rooms and a platform all the way around it. We swam a while and then sat on the platform, on the side away from shore. She sat down right next to me again. I noticed her "built," which was showing pretty well in her bathing suit. We talked a little, rocking our legs back and forth under the platform, and then she put her arm behind me. I figured out that I was expected to do the same, so I did. Then she put her arm around my waist and sort of hugged me. So I hugged her right back. This time when she turned her face to mine, real close, I figured out

that I was supposed to do something. Now I'm not really
that fast kind of guy, but I'm not dumb either, and I'd seen
enough movies to know what comes next. So I leaned over
and let her lips touch mine.

Our lips were rather dry and our lips touching that way
made my hair tingle a little bit, as if maybe some static electricity had passed between us, but otherwise it wasn't too
bad. She didn't scream or slap me and no one saw us so that
was all okay too. We didn't say anything right away. We just
sat there swinging our legs under the platform, but after a
while we started to talk again.

As we sat there, Eddytha told me about her school. She
had friends there, all girls; it was an all-girl-school. I asked
if she participated in team sports. "We don't have sports
teams," she said. "but in gym we play a lot of different sports
and games. I like basketball. I'm pretty good at it because
I'm taller than most of the other girls. I'm usually the center
on our teams, and when we choose sides I'm one of the first
ones picked."

She felt good about that but she added that although
these girls were her friends, she felt strangely apart from
them. The other girls were almost all Catholics who followed the religious practices of the school's church, but since
she and her really best friend, a Jewish girl named Becky,
were not of the same religion, they didn't have to follow the
religious rites of the other girls, and so they were regarded
as somewhat apart.

"It's different with me too," she said, "because my
mother and father divorced, and that's something that my
school's church doesn't approve of. Then my mother married my stepfather, which is also wrong to the other girls.
Once in a while some one of the girls may talk to me about
that. I feel strange about it too, because I also have my real

father. I really love my real father, and I know I'm expected to love my stepfather too. And I do, because it makes my mother happy to have me love him, but I really love my real father more. I feel funny about that. I think I'm expected to love my stepfather just as much. I guess you would say I feel guilty but I can't help loving my real father more." Her voice sounded shaky as she told me this and her eyes looked sort of teary.

I guess this was a real problem in her life. "I'm glad to have friends like you," she told me. "I know that you and Millie don't regard me in this way. I think you understand because you have something like it in your lives too, with your mother a Catholic, married to a Protestant, and your mother is considered to be "out of the church" by other Catholics. She must feel terrible about that."

I said, "She does, but she goes to church anyway; she just can't take the sacraments, like communion, when she goes to Mass. If my father wasn't so stubborn, they could get remarried by a priest and then everything would be okay again. She hopes he will someday agree to do that." She sat there quietly, thinking about all that; not saying anything, but I could understand the thoughts that must have been spinning through her head.

After a while we stopped talking, I took my arm away from around her back. She said, "We ought to go back." We got up, and went back to the boat and headed for shore.

When we reached shore, Millie and Henry, who had also come to the beach with us, wanted to know where we had been, and they wanted to row too, so we all took off in the boat, and they rowed us around for a while until they became tired of it. We told them we had just rowed around a while and sat on the deck of the old bathhouse. That wasn't really a lie because that is what we did. I left out the other part. Then we all went in to shore and changed clothes in the bathhouse there. After a while, Al came along and took us out to the fairgrounds.

The next day was pretty good too. Mrs. Dennison had invited our family to have dinner at the place they had rented on the lake. She and my mother fried chickens and made a lot of other things, so we had a good homemade dinner. Special arrangements were made so we could do that. Uncle Mike took over the ticket booth on the Lindy Loop for my mother, and the Dennisons had Mr. Carsons run the fishpond. My folks loved to play cards, so they started playing Five Hundred with the Dennisons. Eddytha and I decided to take a walk. My mother wouldn't let Millie go with us. She must have suspected something.

It had been raining and was pretty cool. It was almost fall and this was the last fair for us kids. There was still a little rain drizzling away as we put on a coat to take our walk. We walked along the lake for a while. It wasn't all built up. The path turned into the woods and although we could see the lake through the trees, we were really in the woods. There was no one around, and so Eddytha put her arm around my waist again. After a while when I was sure no one was around, I put my arm around her too. I was walking along mostly making comments about some birds, and then about the rain, and then about how dark the woods were, and then she stopped.

She turned in front of me. Oops! I knew what was coming. But you know what she did first. She licked her lips and made them moist. That seemed like a good idea to me so I did too. This time when our lips touched, it felt different. Better somehow. Especially when she didn't pull away right away. And then she tried another kiss, and this time she put both arms around me and really hugged me. Well, that did it. I was feeling hot and funny and then I realized that this kind of kissing was what was meant by "going all the way." Then we went all the way again. I put my arms around her and hugged her, and we kissed with wet lips, and held it as long as we could. I'm glad I had seen it done that way in the movies. Otherwise I wouldn't have known what to do.

We just stood there holding each other thinking maybe we would go all the way again when a stick cracked along the pathway and a man walked by in the opposite direction. He said, "Rainy day," and we mumbled something like that too. We had been caught. I was glad it wasn't anyone we knew. We decided we had better go back before the folks suspected anything.

They were playing cards. I don't think they even missed us. They asked if it were still raining. Millie and Eddytha and I played some rummy, but all the time I was thinking of the funny feeling I had when we kissed and how I wished we could do it again. But, inside the house, I hardly dared look at Eddytha because my mother might suspect that we had been kissing and maybe even that we had hugged too. We went back to the fair later that evening.

Shawano was another so-so fair as far as making money. The weather had turned rainy and cool the last few days, so we didn't draw large crowds to the fair. It was a beautiful area. Fall was setting in and the trees had already started to turn color because it was farther north than most of our other spots. But hat also meant that it was almost Labor Day and school would start the day after.

I saw Eddytha a couple of times after that just to say "hello," but we never had a chance to even touch each other before we left. I wanted to kiss her goodbye, but I never had the chance. A few days later, it was time to leave. Our season with the carnival was over, more than we realized.

Afterward

MY MOTHER WENT BACK HOME WITH US THIS TIME. THE outfit had a few more fairs to go, but she decided she should be with us at our age. Maybe she had learned of my interest in Eddytha. It had been arranged that Uncle Mike would take over my mother's work, keeping the books and other work she did regularly. My uncle still had not found a job. In fact there were more and more layoffs at the factories, and there were many sad stories of people out of work.

We started back to school after Labor Day. This was my second semester in high school. I had decided to be a pharmacist and was taking the courses which would apply toward admission to pharmacy school in college. Fortunately, the courses included enough of the other sciences so that I later found that I was also qualified for pre-med. I liked the sciences and math and did well at that. I was okay in English, except for composition. I had absolutely no ability at writing.

The show played a couple of fairs and then played the fair at Oshkosh, the Winnebago County Fair. Another attraction, The Glass House, had joined the show after Millie and I left for school. The plan was that it would be part of our midway for the remainder of the season, about another month.

The Glass House was on the order of a "fun house." I

learned that you entered by a glass door and walked through a series of corridors separated from each other by plate glass partitions or mirrored walls. One might be going in one direction and find someone going in the opposite direction in the corridor next to you, being separated from each other by these heavy glass partitions. That and mirrors at the end of the sometimes short passageways created a confusing fun-like effect. This led around a corner to a dark hallway with twists and turns, leading into a room outfitted with strange mirrors which distorted your appearance into truly strange and funny-looking shapes. Once you had your fill of viewing the peculiar appearances of yourself and your friend, you entered a wind tunnel which led you back to the midway. I would like to have gone through that Glass House, but I never did.

There was something very serious that happened there one day. This seemed like fun to two teen-aged girls who were following two boys from their school as they decided to try the Glass House. I learned the full story of this over the years from snatches of conversations I overheard between my parents and others.

The boys went through the corridors, the girls following. As they approached the darkened passageway, one of the girls felt strangely warm. She soon became sweaty and hot. She became dizzy and couldn't get her breath. The walls were coming closer to her, closing in on her. She screamed in terror. She became hysterical. She had to get out. At that moment, one of the boys jumped out at her from the darkened passage. In utter panic, she screamed wildly and turned to run, crashing into a mirrored wall, falling backward as shards of glass rained down on her hands and face, leaving her screaming and thrashing on the floor attempting to get up and out of this nightmarish, claustrophobic situation. The boys disappeared. Her friend stood fixed, screaming, in utter disbelief.

The ticket taker acted quickly and ran to help her. He found it difficult to control her and to stop the bleeding of her wounds. There was blood everywhere. The poor girl was dragged out of the Glass House to the front platform where a passing nurse gave immediate aid, removing a shard of glass from one wound and compressing others with towels, handkerchiefs, and other cloths gathered from the quickly assembled crowd, as she acted to stop the flow of blood. Someone ran to the first-aid office at the grandstand area, and an ambulance responded quickly to transport the victim to the hospital.

She had suffered multiple lacerations of these exposed parts of her face, legs, arms, and hands. At the hospital she was sedated and later anesthetized while surgeons sutured her multiple wounds. The wounds did not involve deep structures, and fortunately her eyes had not been injured. However, it was obvious she would have multiple scars, some of which might be seriously disfiguring.

She was hospitalized for observation and was then sent home after a few days, to suffer thereafter the residuals of what should have been an uneventful passage through the Glass House.

The glass house closed down and did not complete its association with the outfit. The fair went on, and in a few hours it would seem superficially as if nothing had happened, which certainly wasn't the case. And certainly too, the young lady who had suffered her first-ever attack of claustrophobia, would live forever with the memory of that fateful moment.

It's difficult to say whether the horrible accident or the worsening economic times were most at fault for the decline in business at that fair. Even the earlier fairs and the city lots which we played that year had not been highly successful financially.

The carnival finished the season and went into winter quarters. There was no southern trip this year. That had been a loser, and this last season was something of a loser too. In fact, business in general had slowed almost everywhere. It seemed that the great era of prosperity which had been enveloping the country for years was now heading into a recession. In fact a lot of people were concerned about business conditions, worrying about their jobs. It wasn't long before their fears were validated.

Something bad happened on October 29th in 1929. People said the stock market "crashed." A lot of people lost a lot of money. It became apparent that this was the beginning of what became known as "The Great Depression." In the next few years it had a profound effect on business throughout the world. As conditions became worse, banks failed. People lost their money when the banks were unable to pay back the money the people had saved in the banks. People lost money in stocks and other investments. Businesses went broke, bankrupt. Factories closed. Jobs were lost. It was not unusual to hear of men who had left home, leaving their families, looking for work, or simply to escape their responsibilities. Some people were literally starving, penniless, thrown out of their homes, reduced to begging and welfare. People became despondent over their losses, even to the extent of committing suicide in some cases.

It was not unexpected when the family of the poor girl who had been injured in the accident in the Glass House brought suit against the show, my dad, and the owner of the Glass House.

} 132 {

It was a surprise to me when I learned that my folks were not able to keep up the payments on the semis. That loan was foreclosed, the trucks sold, and we still owed money on them.

My dad went back to slaughtering hogs for the winter after the show closed.

The big hit came when the Glass House accident case went through the courts and the young girl received a generous award from the jury and the courts. I doubt that any amount of money would be enough to compensate for the tragedy that had befallen this young girl. However, it was an amount which heavily exceeded the insurance coverage for my dad's share of the award. Their debts forced them to sell the carnival.

The proceeds from the forced sale of used carnival equipment is not likely to be comparable to its real value, and it was not. The Lindy Loop was not yet paid for, and although it brought a good price, it was not enough to do much more than pay the unpaid portion of the loan used to purchase it. The Whip was at least six years old, and somewhat deteriorated, so it did not bring a good price, but there was no loan on it to further complicate the situation. Ferris Wheels do not deteriorate much, so it was in good shape, but with every other outfit already having their own Ferris Wheel, the market for it among other carnival owners was not very exciting. It sold under market price. We owed nothing on it. The used tents, poles, canvas, banners, shows, trailers and wagons, the Fordson and the transformer wagon and cables and everything else all went for bargain prices.

I couldn't believe it when I learned all this. The carnival was gone. The show broke up. My dad's dream and all the work my mother and dad had put into it was gone.

The outfit broke up. Uncle Henry sold the Chair-O-

Plane and his other carnival stuff. The Rexalls, Dennisons, Normans, and "Dutch" Rogers hooked on with other shows. Mr. Haywood with his Tilt-A-Whirl and John De-Jung with his Merry-Go-Round did the same. Jackie Coyle and Erma retired after selling their historic collections. Charlie Peterson went into another type of wrestling show business. A lot of the Carnies went down to "Gibtown" in Florida, the town known as a Carnie wintertime hangout, to see what might be in the wind for them. Others went looking for jobs, which were more scarce every day. The "Dog and Pony Show" went looking for other bookings. Mongo went back to Milwaukee. Al Beuse stayed with us and worked with my dad. Uncle Louie took a job as a used-car salesman. Uncle Mike got a job as a butcher in a meat market. Uncle Henry worked with my father butchering hogs.

Eddytha sent me a scarf for Christmas, and I sent her some candy. It was years before I saw her again, and then only long enough for a few hugs and a bit of smooching. I hope she is married to a nice guy. She deserves a good person.

Our world had changed. But all the world was changing. The financial depression struck everyone in some way or other. Even at that time, we were just getting into the depths of it, and it would become worse before it got better. We and everyone so affected did the best they could, and some could do nothing about it. Many men stood selling apples from a box on street corners in the big cities, in the hope of making a few dollars to sustain them, or turned to the soup lines in desperation for a meal. Some men left home, abandoning their responsibilities. Some committed suicide.

We were a long time in recovering. All the world went into a prolonged business depression. It took about ten years to get back to what economists considered normal times.

We coped as best we could. My mother and father worked at various jobs to make a go of it. Millie and I eventually had jobs too to help survive, she in a dime store, while I solicited magazine subscriptions door to door until I landed a job as an errand boy in a clothing store for twenty-five cents an hour. But we made it.

Millie later married an Army man who unfortunately became a World War II casualty, battle fatigue, eventually leading to alcoholism. This ended in divorce. A second marriage to an army officer gave her a nice life.

Eventually, I was able to go to college and medical school. My parents struggled with a variety of occupations, proving their resiliency and adaptability to the changes in their fortune, eventually gaining esteem and financial security.

Even so, it was not easy for us. I can recall the weeks before my third year in medical school, when it seemed that my parents could not afford to keep me in school, although I had part-time jobs to help pay expenses. My father had started a little business, recapping used tires. At that time of further crisis, my mother started to work as an "Avon Lady," selling cosmetics house to house at first, later from our home after she had an established clientele. I continued school and work.

As I write this, it is now eighty years later, a long way back to the days of the carnival. Those days seem unreal after all that has transpired. I have trouble believing all that did occur at that time. I guess I'm somewhat proud of the fact that we survived. As far as I can tell, it didn't hurt us to struggle. Some say it can improve your character. I don't know. I hope so.

I do know that my life had taken some interesting and

sometimes difficult turns, ultimately with a happy ending. Few can best me at this age of ninety-four years in terms of longevity, coupled with having had a great marriage, plentifully endowed with children, grandchildren, and great grandchildren, as well as a career which many say was noteworthy in terms of the work I performed, and which I know has given me financial reward as well. I have been most fortunate that the Good Lord enabled me to serve society in one of the most gratifying of occupations.

I am also aware that when I see or hear of a carnival, there occurs some kind of a little flip-flop in my blood flow. Whenever I possibly can, I sneak over to the outfit to see what's going on. It must be that "Carnie blood." It's hard to get rid of that quickening of your heartbeat, even if you want to, and even if you despise certain aspects of the carnival life of those days. It's "in my genes." I continue with a lot of good memories of those days, and a few bad ones. At heart, I continue to relate closely to that life, but I no longer want to live it. Today, I realize that deep down inside, I had found the carnival life an interesting and enjoyable way of life. And so, as time goes on, I'm forced to recognize that this "passage" in my life did give me the unique opportunity to experience this unusual way of life, which also served to remind me of how fortunate I have been to survive the unsavory aspects of such a life as it was in those days and times. Those experiences have probably helped me in many ways in life. I'm glad they are behind me, and yet, I treasure the memories of those days. They are all a part of me. In that way, I'm still a "Carnie."

Today

Now, I write this memoir at the age of ninety-four, having spent fifty-six years in what some might refer to as a successful lifetime practice of orthopaedic surgery, beginning in 1947 in South Bend, Indiana, and after fifty-six years starting in 1943 in Chicago, of a supremely satisfying married life with a beautiful (in all respects) wife. She was also bountiful in terms of the nine good kids, twenty-four grandchildren, and subsequently eight great-grandchildren with which she endowed me. My wife has passed on. I am retired, with reasonable health to enable me to pursue some interests for which I did not have time enough in my working years.

Sports, spectator types, yes. Football, baseball, tennis, basketball, golf, and now even lacrosse, hockey, and soccer interest me. During my active years, I had the opportunity to indulge this interest by combining it with my part-time occupation as orthopaedic surgeon to the athletic teams at the University of Notre Dame for thirty-five years, a position which gave me some recognition as one of the earlier sports-medicine physicians. Active sports? I knew I could develop a good game of golf when I retired and had time to work at it. Wrong! I didn't count on the progressive loss of strength, coordination, stamina, and even vision that comes with the golden years. Can't even see the ball to follow its flight most

CARNIE

of the time. I'm within an inch of giving up completely on golf.

Games? I'm trying to catch up on modern bridge. So many nuances, all meant to make it a more exact game. If only I could remember all of those simple rules that I agreed upon with my partner to help us win consistently, but the old mind has some moth-eaten holes to screw me up, and even bad card hands interfere with having a good game of bridge.

The Arts? I can see well enough to enjoy the visual arts: movies, and theatre, ballet, paintings, and sculpture. I enjoy the scenes, the colors, the music, the dance, the virtuosity, but I must now add my complaint about my ears. They no longer hear well; even with the best of aids, I'm still lost when it comes to listening to speech, whether it be TV, movies, or theatre.

Reading? I'm catching up on all kinds, fiction and not. So many interesting things out there beside medicine. Science and the memoirs and biographies of great men especially interest me.

Conversation? Okay in a reasonably quiet room sitting next to my opposite number, especially if of my age, one who speaks at a normal pace. Young people? No! They talk so fast I have to stop them, have them slow down so I can distinguish one word from the next.

I'll tell you what I do enjoy. My family and close friends. It's great to know what's going on in their lives. Talking with the younger folks is different. I struggle to interject a comment or two when I can force a word between theirs during their rapid-fire conversations. I especially love it when my kids slip up and relate some incident of which I was never informed while they were growing up. My good wife, Bunny, saw to it that I was not thereby stressed, and the rod was spared. And yet, they were not spoiled. She took care of the situation with soft words and the softer her voice became, the greater the attention the kids paid to her admonitions. That's when she really meant business. Don't test her. The punishments were not physical, but they bruised the freedom and ego of the privileged class of youth.

Time with friends is now available. Friends and a few drinks make easy and enjoyable conversation, especially when with select company. We avoid the snares of religion, politics, and pseudo science. Unfortunately, every conversation turns to who died or is dying, requiring us to interrupt our personal litany of aches and pains which will ultimately ground us, six feet under This select company has been narrowed by selection, age, disability, and death. Those who remain are ever so much more dear.

The carnival of today has really grabbed my interest. Now with enough time I have begun to pursue my submerged interest in the life I left behind in my youth. Now I can go to the fair or to the carnival lot and completely enjoy those beautiful steeds circling by to the tune of Merry-Go-Round organ music. As my interest increased, I acquainted myself with the carnival workers and their bosses for details of their lives. They accepted me as one who had been "with it." They spoke freely and sometimes eagerly in telling their stories, since I was one of them. I was a "Carnie." They filled me in on the details of the changes which had occurred and of the big business that the carnival world had become. This was in marked contrast to that carnival world I had left behind.

The Carnival of Today

As all things change, so too has the world of carnivals, and in this case, for the better. The carnival world has been altered by many modern influences. These included technological developments, safety and legal considerations, expanded and innovative feats of engineering, the application of business-like efficiency, and a more paternalistic interest on the part of management in the care and feeding of its Carnie workforce.

The keenness of competition in the diverse world of entertainment was instrumental in this drive for ever bigger and better showmanship. Altered consciousness eliminated the dishonesty of the "grifters" with their gimmicks and gaffs of the concessions which once lined the midways. The carnival world had cleaned up its act. The "grifters" are gone.

The changes in morality in the business of games were the result of several factors. For one, payoffs to officials became an excessive expense to pave the way for these gambling concessions. Too many palms had to be plastered with greenbacks to avoid the law and complaints. Second, the thinking public had become aware that the joints had gaffs which did not give them an even chance to win. Third, the competition of the large permanent amusement parks forced the carnivals to present an equally clean and honest form of entertainment. And finally, the carnivals became aware that if they were to return to communities and fairs for repeat engagements, they had best maintain healthy relationships with their customer base. And so, carnivals today present honest games and concessions. In fact, the philosophy among many concessionaires is that everyone gets a prize for trying. It may not be much, maybe just an inexpensive prize referred to as slum; but there you have a winner, a satisfied customer. Some of the smaller outfits may break the rules on some games, and even in some larger outfits, there may be some simple gaffs like wide-based milk bottles to be knocked off a rack only with great difficulty. However, the smart concessionaire also sees to it that there are enough winners of the better prizes to entice others to play the games. As a result, today one sees many people on the midway carrying their small "slum" prizes as well as those carrying their large stuffed animals. Everyone's happy to be among the lucky ones.

There are few shows with the carnivals today. They have been replaced with walk-through fun houses or glassed maze types of attractions. Again it is the competition of other sources of entertainment and the altered consciousness of the politically correct that have changed the scene.

Television has caused one of the main changes, with its freely available boxing, wrestling, and other shows. Specialty productions such as the magic and illusion shows of David Copperfield and even the gymnastic performance arts such as the Cirque du Soleil can be seen on TV, or in specially staged productions. Even the presentation and handling of reptiles, such as the adventurous presentations of the late Steve Irwin, the unfortunate South African crocodile wrestler, who died when the barb of a sting-ray penetrated his chest, are better presented on television than at the old carnival shows.

Among the last vestiges of true outdoor showmanship were the Ten-in-One shows. They were once a standard fixture with both carnivals and circuses. Many of these presented what were known as "freaks," those unfortunate individuals who had suffered embryonic birth defects and bodily malformations. It is no longer in good taste to make a show of those who are thus handicapped. These shows have faded away.

Probably the last surviving traveling Ten-in-One show is the one presented by the legendary showman, Ward Hall, and his partner, Chris Christ, but it is one made up today of performance acts rather than presentation of the handicapped. Today's shows present the fire-eaters, sword-swallowers, knife-throwers, ventriloquists, contortionists, and others. All of this has changed, it too for the better.

Newer technological and engineering principles have been adapted to the mechanics of the carnival rides to provide an ever-more-exhilarating experience to the riders. Any number of machines now transport the passengers in all directions: whirling, swinging, twisting, turning, flying, throwing them in all directions as they experience the thrill of the ride. In some, they virtually overcome the effect of gravity by the application of centrifugal force, such as in the Tornado. Other rides swing and carry the strapped-in rider in a vertical direction through an ever increasing arc eventually swinging him upside down and high above the ground in the ride known as the Ring of Fire. Other riders are sent spinning in a revolving car while being flung out on the end of a long radial spoke while traveling in a circle coupled with ascending and descending sequences as in the "Scrambler." Still others are carried aloft by a vertical wheel reaching unheard of heights in today's "Ferris Wheel."

The Ferris Wheel was invented by George Ferris Jr. for the 1889 World's Fair in Chicago, to provide a sensational attraction to rival the Eiffel Tower in Paris. Actually, as early as the year 1620, a Peter Mundy, traveling in Turkey, reported and sketched a hand-operated, vertically oriented Wheel as well as a Merry-Go-Round with seats for children.

However, Ferris's Wheel was the first large mechanically powered such ride, and it was truly an engineering marvel in its day. It was 264 feet to the top and could carry 2160 passengers. My father's Wheel was 45 feet high; the tallest Ferris Wheel in those days reached fifty-five feet. Both Wheels were portable and had been developed by William E. Sullivan of the Eli Bridge Company.

Today's monstrous "Giant Wheel" reaches one hundred feet in height. Erecting a wheel of that height, which is transportable, became practical only after hydraulic principles were applied to the carnival world. Hydraulics make it possible to lift massively heavy loads with minimal equipment. As a result, with the help of this and other applied engineering principles the midways are now filled with the wide variety of rides, providing thrills enough for even the most daring riders.

Also impressive are the engineering principles utilized in erecting, dismantling, and moving the rides. Most of the rides are now racked on a base platform with that platform mounted on a trailer ingeniously designed allowing the ride to virtually unfold from this base. Dismantling the ride is a similar but reverse process. In many cases an entire ride may be fitted onto one trailer.

American manufacturers of these rides are meeting stiff competition from foreign countries, principally European countries. The purchase of such equipment constitutes a considerable investment, some rides costing well over

$1 million. Although they are built with portability in mind, they must also be durable. The frequent erection and dismantling of the rides increases the wear and tear on them, requiring periodic repair and rehabilitation. This is usually done at the winter quarters of the outfit, but it may require return to the factory or to companies specializing in such work. Proper maintenance of the rides is necessary to keep them safe for riders.

Safety is an area of serious concern in the carnival world. Accidents do happen but many are preventable. The larger outfits have prepared manuals for their workers, familiarizing them with measures to be undertaken to prevent accidents and injuries and the actions to be undertaken should such occur. Both the customers of the carnival and the carnival workers must be protected.

Among the well-managed outfits, such as the Skerbeck Brothers Shows, an outfit based on fifty rides, there are established and detailed programs for safety. They, like the larger outfits, build their program on ride and equipment inspection, on its maintenance, and on employee training and customer education.

Rides are subject to safety inspections regularly. New rides must pass government safety inspections before approval is granted for their use. They also undergo an annual inspection by certified inspectors. All rides are also inspected after each setup or move, by certified officials, and are also inspected daily by one or more certified safety personnel of the carnival organization. The superintendent for each ride performs daily inspection, recording his findings on a checklist of safety features to certify compliance with these safety measures before customers are allowed on the ride. The best of the outfits have their own qualified safety personnel to inspect the rides regularly to ensure further safety.

Qualification for certification of these inspectors requires training and examination by the National Association of Amusement Ride Officials, (NAARSCO) as well as by the American Industry Manufacturers and Suppliers (AIMS).

The rides are also constructed, operated, and maintained under standards set by the F24 Committee of the American Society of Testing and Materials (ASTM).

Customer safety is also dependent on devices to secure the customer in his seat. It also requires consumer cooperation.

In spite of these measures accidents may occur, 60 percent of which are estimated to be due to failure of riders to observe the safety measures in place. Statistics available through the National Electronic Injury Surveillance System (NEISS) reveal an estimate of an annual average of 3,500 injuries related to the mobile carnival rides over a long period of years, from 1987 to 2005, with twelve related deaths during that time.

The carnival owners protect themselves against these incidents with insurance. The costs are high, some carnivals paying hundreds of thousands of dollars for their protection annually.

Further insurance is carried for other reasons. The big outfits have a fleet of their own trucks to move the equipment from one location to the next. Insurance on such fleets is a very costly item. Workmen's compensation insurance and insurance against fire, theft, and other events are necessary, as in any business.

The use of drugs and alcohol may also affect safety in the operation of carnival equipment, rides, and trucks. Most outfits have a zero tolerance policy on this. Outfits that have their own fleets, have their truckers as well as other employees undergo drug testing when they are hired and periodically at other times.

Other background checks are made on employees to avoid harboring criminals. These outfits have their own personnel departments, just as any major business does.

There is greater concern for the help today than in the past. Full-time employees in the big outfits may be housed in bunkhouses, trailers composed of multiple bunks or one-room compartments, not unlike those on our trains, complete with washing, bathing, and toilet facilities but also with facilities for light cooking. The employees are usually provided with some degree of uniform, one or more articles of clothing and with facilities for laundering of these articles, which are to be worn on duty. This is to identify them as employees and to create the discipline that comes with uniformity.

Cleanliness and neatness are required of the help. Most outfits take pride in the cleanliness of their attractions and their midways. Some, such as The Butler Shows, present themselves as "the cleanest carnival in the West." A real point of pride.

The carnival life is not attractive to all people. Carnies are almost always on the move. Family life and home life are rather stilted. The pay scale for the help is in the minimum wage area and benefits are negligible. There are no health benefits, although the Outdoor Amusement Business Association has individual health and life policies available; the Carnie has only the beneficence of the carnival owner to fall back onto if disaster strikes. They are of course covered by workmen's compensation insurance, for work-related conditions. They have no pension plans, but most employees will probably receive a season's-end bonus, probably little more than just enough to get one back to one's home base during the off-season.

The matter of finding willing and suitable workers is done in various ways, one of the more frequent means is that of arranging with agencies who contract with individuals for this work. Not infrequently these workers are from foreign countries, where jobs are few and which do not even compare in compensation with that of these indentured employees whose transportation, visas, taxes, and salaries are arranged by contract, with the agency. The agency is compensated by the carnival management for these services. Mexican workers are among those imported. They gain employment on a temporary visa in the US. Australians are another source, a preferred one since they speak English fluently. Others are from Europe, the Caribbean Islands, and elsewhere. At times these agencies arrange for work forces only for the short period of the moves from one spot to another.

Moving these big carnival outfits is a major undertaking. A big fair, like the North Carolina State Fair, may have more than one hundred rides on site. This would require many trucks and trailers to transport the rides and equipment. The largest outfits have their own fleet of trucks, tractors, and semis to make the moves. These are subject to many legalities including periodic inspections by the Department of Transportation. Trains are no longer part of the pattern of moving these outfits. The switch to motorized shows began in the late 1920's, and by the '70s, movement by rail was almost extinct. The Royal American Shows, which once moved exclusively by rail, owning their own railroad cars, gave up moving by rail in the '70s. A number of their railroad cars are now museum pieces at the showrooms of the International Independent Showmen's Association (IISA) in Gibsonton, Florida. The Strates Shows are the last of the outfits to move by rail.

The IISA is a fraternal and trade organization for all persons and businesses associated with the outdoor amusement world. Their headquarters are in Gibsonton. Here they have a large clubhouse decorated colorfully with carnival posters and paraphernalia. It houses a meeting room, a banquet room complete with dance floor and bandstand, and a large bar and recreation room. They also sponsor a retirement facility and cemetery for long-time members of the association. Their major activity takes place in their adjacent and large convention center. This houses their annual trade show, the IISF Trade Show and Extravaganza, at which all organizations and businesses associated with the world of outdoor amusements are invited to present their products and interests. This is also associated with an annual banquet and awards ceremony lending a social aspect to the occasion.

The IISA is also in the process of developing a museum devoted to the world of carnivals. The building has been completed, and IISA is currently awaiting funding for the interior furnishings to display the articles which they are collecting. These will present the history and accompaniments of this interesting outdoor amusement world.

Gibsonton is not far from Tampa. It is the stopping place for many show-people, as a winter haven for some, but for others, Gibsonton is home, either as their permanent residence, or as a retirement home. I'm told that at one time the resident population included many from the sideshows, midgets, people with various abnormalities, and others, so that it was not surprising to see some of these unusual people on the streets of Gibsonton going about their everyday lives. Along the streets and in their yards one can see evidence of the presence of Carnies: their carnival wagons, signs of their professions, magicians, animal trainers, and others.

When the outfits go into winter quarters, the residents return to "Gib-town." Carnies who do not have homes elsewhere are likely to descend on the town and its area to spend the winter in a comfortable and affordable region. Some of the southern outfits have their winter season headquarters in the area. There are also numerous companies specializing in the rehabilitation of carnival rides and equipment located here.

I visited Ward Hall there. Ward is a veteran showman. He and his partner, Chris Christ (pronounced Crist), live there with their long-time friend and associate, Pete Terhune, a midget. They occupy a rambling one-story home, complete with pool, just off U.S. Route 41, adjacent to an environmental preserve. A bunk-house trailer for housing the members of his show sits in the yard. In his neighbor's yard is a trailer proclaiming it to be that of a magician; down the street was a lady who had a dog show; and at the local restaurant and bar, Showtown USA, I met a lady lion tamer.

The home is filled with mementos of their careers in the outdoor show business, which has been most varied and colorful. Ward is a veteran of outdoor shows. He and Chris, have put on many varieties of these outdoor shows. His tent shows have included freak and performance-type shows, vaudeville-type variety and girl shows, minstrel shows, snake shows, and many Ten-in-One shows.

Ward was a full-time circus sideshow performer by age fourteen. Now at age 78, he restricts himself to one Ten-in-One show, putting it on the road for several months in the summer and fall, hitting the big fairs with his troupe of performers. In years past these shows usually displayed what were then called freaks, such as the bearded lady, the four-legged man, Siamese twins, and others. They also had some fakes like the two-headed baby in a jar of preservative, constructed by Ward from two dolls, one of whom lost its head. Ward Hall has been especially prominent as a showman.

At times he had several of these large tent shows on the road at the same time. He himself in his earlier years was part of these very shows. At various times he had been ventriloquist, magician, fire-eater, clown, sword-swallower, bingo caller, snake handler, and in one act he juggled dumbbells while climbing a ladder of swords. He had been front talker and grinder, singer, musician, property hand, ringmaster, actor and producer of a television show, and even the target man for a knife-thrower.

His partner, Chris, was more the business man but had also done his time as ringmaster and front speaker. Pete, the midget, was a talented man who was a steady attraction on the bally platform. He was also a performer with acts such as sword swallowing, fire eating, working the snake pit, and fitting in wherever needed in the Ten-in-One shows.

The days of these Ten-in-One shows have apparently all but passed. Ward explained that his is the last of these shows on the traveling circuit. The shows no longer display freaks. Those afflicted ones made a bare living while being shown, and with the changes in social welfare, they no longer need expose themselves to the curious, an occupation they did not really wish for themselves. And so that too represents the passing of an era. Only the performance type of show persists.

We never had a minstrel show with our outfit, but that too was considered degrading and was replaced with other types of shows such as Rock and Roll shows. Today even those are fading. They have gone upscale in some areas. The magicians today put on grandiose productions, real show business, commanding large audiences in theatres at advanced prices. So too go the variety shows, the burlesque shows, the girlie shows, the wrestling shows, the acrobatic shows, and other performing-arts shows. The snake shows, the displays of curios, and strange animal shows are now relegated to zoos, museums, and television shows.

Concessions are now of many types; novelty stands, photo studios, food, and games. The novelty joints sell the merchandise you relate to the fairs; balloons, stuffed animals, inscribed "T" shirts, your favorite sport team's baseball caps, pennants, and the like. The food concessions or "grab joints" feature mainly quick foods. An extensive variety is presented, including the time-honored sugar floss or cotton candy, taffy apples, hot dogs, cone cakes, hot tamales, ice cones, and more. Today the choices are much wider and frequently present new favorites, including pizza, corn dogs, fried pickles, meatball sandwiches, deep fried candy bars, elephant ears, and others.

The games today are either pure games of chance, or they may require the skills of throwing darts, shooting basketballs or baseballs, shooting guns, hammering the striker, tossing rings, and other activities. Other games are electronic, such as the horse-racing layouts. These and several other games are sophisticated electronic layouts which require a substantial investment on the part of the concessionaire, some costing over $100,000. It is good to say, however, that the games are no longer tainted by the gaffs and the grifters of the earlier era.

Carnivals today are really big business. A large carnival may handle millions of dollars at a large state fair. *Carnival* Magazine in January, 2008, reported that the show, Powers Great American Midways, arranged for the showing of 113 rides at the 2007 North Carolina State Fair, making over $4 million for the fair.

The investment and expenses of a carnival outfit are equally great. Even a mid-sized outfit such as Skerbeck Brothers pays out a quarter million dollars annually for insurance alone.

Ticket sales at carnivals are now done most efficiently by selling not one but books of tickets or coupons, maybe fifteen to twenty-five for $12–$25, or even an all day or part day pass. Many of the attractions will require several coupons under this system.

Carnivals are no longer the loosely organized outfits of yesterday. Some of the larger organizations have over 200 rides available, operating several shows on the road at one time. Most outfits are under corporate structure, but today even larger corporations have developed, buying up and incorporating other outfits, even as many as six prominent carnivals having been bought up by the Cyprus Investment Group.

And so the traveling carnival survives. With all the changes they are generally bigger and better. The smaller outfits struggle to make it. They get the smaller, less desirable venues, as a result of which their income does not allow some of the niceties, the uniforms, the frequent drug testing, the housing, the wages and security attendant with the large outfits.

One of the largest of the traveling carnivals is The Strates Shows. It is the last show to travel by rail. It has its own railroad cars and requires almost sixty rail cars and more than twenty-five trucks to transport its many rides, games, and concessions, as well as its over 400 employees, traveling over 7,000 miles in a seven-month season. The show can provide 50 to 70 rides for an event.

The Outdoor Amusement Business Association (OABA) is the business-political organization for both circuses and carnivals. It also serves all businesses, organizations, and persons with interests in this area. In the carnival world alone, there are approximately three hundred and fifty outfits of which the larger carnivals are capable of operating several midways around the country simultaneously. The OABA concerns itself with problems affecting the industry: legal changes, taxes, quality assessment programs, consumer safety, animal issues, etc. It does the lobbying for the industry where necessary.

The OABA has also been instrumental in the development of ride safety standards together with the American Society of Testing and Materials' F24 Committee.

The Showmen's League, another organization for the outdoor amusement world, is a fraternal organization established in 1913 with Colonel William F. Cody (Buffalo Bill) as its first president. Their stated mission is described as being "dedicated to service and fellowship, to men and women show-people." They are a fraternal organization serving carnies and circus workers and their families. Their activities include "providing scholarships, financial aid, memorial services, and the promotion of the mutual welfare of their members and all show-people in good times and bad." One of their annual activities is a gala party for handicapped children. Another is the annual participation in the Gibtown, IISA Trade Show in February, and an annual dinner in Las Vegas. They are truly a social and fraternal organization, extending their benefits to the families and members of the Showmen's League through their fund-raising activities. Their big social event of the year is held annually in Las Vegas in cooperation with the OABA, and the International Association of Fairs and Exhibitions (IAFE).

They maintain the "Showmen's Rest" in Woodlawn cemetery in Chicago as a final resting place for their members, including those who may have died indigent. They too are assured of a final resting place.

I know today's carnivals only by visiting and interviewing the owners, the showmen, and the help. In doing so, I have met many interesting people and made some good friends. One of the realities of today is the level of education among carnies. Many of the show owners and probably most of the upper echelon players are college educated, as are many at the lower levels. Others have had a high school education. Many are traveling with families when convenient, just as we did, but with better facilities for living, some with glamorous motor homes, truly homes on wheels.

The ownership and top management of the outfits are very often being continued along family lines, sons, daughters, and in-laws, some continue today even into their fifth generation, as with the Skerbeck Brothers Shows. In fact it appears now that there will be a sixth generation involved soon.

Butler Amusements, Inc., a California based show, was started in 1970 by George "Bud" Butler. This became a family business. When George passed on, his son, "Butch" Butler, took over the outfit. His daughter, Tami Butler Quint, is Office Manager at Winter Quarters; her husband, Ron, is Head of Transportation. Daughter Kelley Butler operates the main unit office. Daughter Kris Butler Brajevich and husband, Mick, operate the Washington and Oregon unit of the show. Daughter Jill Butler Moyer and husband, Lance, operate another of their large carnival units. Son Sean Murphy Butler is attending college and is another family member likely to join the business, truly a family business.

In this evolutionary process, carnivals have become more efficient, more business-like in their operation, larger, more diverse in their rides and concessions, cleaner, safer, and more considerate of the help and of their customers.

And so the show goes on, and better than in my day. I wonder now how we got by as we did. It was an interesting trip while it lasted, and unfortunate as was the ending of my personal childhood experience with carnivals, I do believe that it too was for the best. I can't imagine what my life would have been if I had followed in my father's footsteps. He tried hard, but it just wasn't meant to be. Nevertheless, in one way or another, I learned a lot from his experiences. I'm sure the result has been a better life for me. I learned a lot from that carnival experience. I don't miss the carnival days. There is no desire to return to those days. There were the high spots, but finally there came the low spot. And when I do stop to think of those days, I have more good than bad memories and there is an occasional sense of nostalgia for the days when I was "with it." I think I'll just hang on to the pleasant memories of those days. I prefer those and so I will let it rest there, but I continue to feel the lure. I'm still a "Carnie."

Bibliography

THE FOLLOWING REFERENCES WERE SOURCES CONSULTED to amplify certain aspects of this work:

Allport, Allen. *Great American Presidents*. Philadelphia: Chelsea House Publishers, 2004.

Author/editor. *George Ferris*. Amusement Business, One Hundredth Anniversary Collector's Edition. City: Publisher, 1994; Nov: 12: 20.

Feinberg, Barbara Silberdick B. *Franklin Roosevelt*. Danbury, Conn.: Children's Press, 2005.

Goga, Vicky. *One for the Record Books*, Carnival Magazine. City: Publisher, January, 2008: 16–17.

Hall, Ward. *Struggles and Triumphs of a Modern Day Showman. Sarasota, Fla.:* Carnival Publishers of Sarasota, 1981.

Lambert, David and the Diogram Group. *The Field Guide to Geology*. Facts in Full. City: Publisher, 1932.

McKennon, Joe. *A Pictorial History of the American Carnival*. Sarasota, Fla.: Carnival Publishers of Sarasota, 1972.

Murek, Barabara W. *Geology, a Self Teaching Guide*. New York: John Wiley and Sons, 2001.

Parks, Peggy J. *The Great Depression*. Farmington Hills, Mich.: Kielhaven Press, 2004.

Prelesnik, Mike. *Skerbeck Brothers Shows*. Carnival Magazine. Salisbury, North Carolina, *Carnival* Magazine Publishers, Jan. 2008: 5–7.

Sloat, Warren. *1929, America before the Crash*. New York: Macmillan Publishing, 1979.

Terkel, "Studs." *Hard Times, an Oral History of the Great Depression*. New York: Pantheon Books, 1970.

Ramona, the song, was written by L. Wolfe Gilbert, music by Mabel Wayne in 1927.

Web Sites:

OABA.org/01media/html, safety and injury statistics. Accessed 9/2/2009.

CPSC.gov/Library/Amus2004.pdf for injury statistics. Accessed 9/3/2009.

DNR.wi.gov/org/land/er/sna/sna283.htm. Dells of the Wisconsin

River. Accessed 7/5/07.

Index

CARNIE

Little Johnny, 8–12,
Lombardo, Guy, 115

Madison, Wis., 7, 77–80,
    122–23
Mafia, 37
mark, 45, 105
Menominee, Wis., 41, 89
Mercer, Bob, 2933, 52;
    Wanda (his wife), 29–33,
    52
Merriwell, Frank, 60
Milwaukee, Wis., 134
Mix, Tom (screen actor), 54
Mongo, 118–21
Monroe, Wis., 66–67, 75,
    112, 122,
Moran, "Bugs," 99
Moyer, Jill Butler, 154
Moyer, Lance, 154
Muncie, Ind., 42
Muriel Abbott Dancers, 85
Mussolini, Benito, 100

National Association of
    Amusement Ride
    Officials (NAARSCO),
    145
National Electric Injury
    Surveillance System
    (NEISS), 145
New York Yankees, 100

Normans (workers at
    carnival; husband is
    John), 13, 26, 44, 47, 52,
    80, 106; Johnny (son),
    43–44, 80–82, 87, 113–14;
    Charlie (son), 44, 80,
    113–14; Grandma, 89
North Carolina State Fair,
    147, 151
Notre Dame, University of,
    95, 137

Our Gang comedy, 54–55
Our Lady of Mount Carmel
    Catholic Church, 60
Outdoor Amusement
    Business Association
    (OABA), 146, 152–53

Pathe News Reel, 55
Pennsylvania Railroad
    Station, 95
Peterson, Charlie (worker
    at carnival), 26, 42–43,
    134
Pettits (workers at carnival;
    husband is Art), 26, 41,
    52, 81, 87; Tom (their
    son), 41; Art (son), 41–
    42, 114–15
Pittsburgh, Pa., 7
Portage, Wis., 41, 79–80, 87